D1403186

EMPOWERING
HOUSTONIANS
FOR **100** YEARS

HOUSTON PUBLIC LIBRARY
1904 - 2004

100 Years - 100 Stories
by
Betty Trapp Chapman

FOREWORD

The Houston Public Library celebrates its Centennial in 2004. With the theme, "Empowering Houstonians for 100 Years," the Library is commemorating a century of service. This photographic history of our library facilities and of the people associated with library services brings to life our past and the important role Houston Public Library has played in the history of our city.

And what a history that has been. Paralleling the growth of the city, the Houston Public Library has evolved from a single library located downtown serving a population of 66,113 to the library system we have today with a Central Library comprising the Jesse Jones and Julia Ideson Buildings and the Clayton Center for Genealogical Research, 35 branch libraries, and a library at the Children's Museum—now serving a population of two million. And as the population has grown, so the collections have grown from those first 2,400 books owned by the Houston Lyceum in 1878 to the four million items—books, videos, DVDs, compact discs, books on tape and CDs—which we have today. And with that growth came innovation in library services. It was very early in the history of the Library that collections were placed in schools and other deposit locations convenient to readers. Today the Library reaches into the community electronically, with over four million visits to the Library's website and two million information database searches annually.

In some ways, the Library has changed considerably over the past century. Go into any of our libraries today and you will find our customers using computers, browsing the catalogue, searching online, researching electronic databases, writing their resumes, and reading e-books. Many customers access these services 24/7 from the convenience of their homes and offices. And yet the Library has stayed the same over the past century. We still provide a strong collection of books, magazines, and audiovisual materials. We continue our commitment to customer service and community involvement. A multitude of programs and services are available through community partnerships, just as they were in the early part of the twentieth century. Story times, literacy programs, teen services, and computer classes are just a few of the many services to be found in today's Houston Public Library. All of this comes with the same high-quality customer service from friendly staff members that the Library has always been proud to provide.

As our society grows in size and diversity, and life is increasingly complex, the Houston Public Library, as a source of information, remains committed to empowering the lives of all Houstonians now and in the future.

Barbara A. B. Gubbin
Director of Libraries

ACKNOWLEDGMENTS

The idea for a photographic history to commemorate the centennial of the Houston Public Library was first discussed at a meeting of the Centennial Committee in November 2002. As the project evolved, it received support from many persons whose help was invaluable. I am indebted to Joel Draut, the library's photographic archivist, who went the extra mile in locating and reproducing photographs; to Audrey Crawford, whose sharp eye and editing expertise lent clarity to the words; to librarian Roland Lemonius, who applied his considerable computer skills in developing the compact disc accompanying this book; to Centennial Committee members Mary Frances Townsend and Marje Harris, who efficiently collected information from the branch libraries; to the staff of the Texas Room, who patiently retrieved boxes and boxes of materials for my research; and to Syma Zerkow, whose counsel and encouragement kept me on track.

All of the photographs in *100 Years-100 Stories* are from the photographic collections of the Houston Metropolitan Research Center unless otherwise noted. I want to thank Paul Hester of Hester + Hardaway for allowing us to use his photographs of the branch libraries.

Finally the Houston Public Library is indebted to Houston Endowment, Inc. for continuing its generous support of the library by underwriting the centennial's historical projects, including this photographic history and various exhibits during the year.

As the Houston Public Library moves into its second century, it invites you to become a part of its future.

Betty Trapp Chapman

100 YEARS

On the evening of March 2, 1904, a gala crowd gathered to formally dedicate an impressive new building at the corner of McKinney Avenue and Travis Street. It was the Houston Lyceum and Carnegie Library – the first free public library in Houston. The building was the realization of a longtime dream for thousands of Houstonians. It culminated over fifty years of efforts to bring literary culture to the city. In the next 100 years, the Houston Lyceum and Carnegie Library would evolve into the Houston Public Library and continue to transform to meet the needs of Houston's dynamic growth.

The history of the Houston Public Library began in the first decade of Houston's existence. In the 1840s, Houstonians made various attempts to organize a subscription library to support debating societies in the city. The members of the societies typically were young attorneys, businessmen, and journalists. They met regularly for lively debates on such topics as "Ought dueling to be punished as a capital crime?" and "Have theatres an immoral tendency?" To provide resource material for these debates, they established the Houston Circulating Library and maintained it informally, without a permanent facility.

In 1854 the Houston Lyceum organized and slowly evolved over the next decades into the first Houston public library. It grew a book collection through membership fees and book donations and within three years owned almost eight hundred books. The Lyceum claimed that it was "desirous that the young men of the city should read from the volumes…and thereby improve themselves." Membership was limited to dues-paying white males. Interestingly, one of the Lyceum debates at this time was: "Are women capable of the same mental improvement as men?" No record exists of the outcome of this exercise, but the Lyceum continued to deny women the use of the library for another three decades.

In spite of periodic public offerings of debates and lectures, the Lyceum struggled with finances and facilities. Moving the library to the Banqueting Hall of the recently built Market House in 1878 seemed to breathe new life into the organization. Its library grew to twenty-four hundred books. The librarian reported that the books most in demand were works of fiction, history, and poetry.

In an effort to resolve its financial problems, in 1887 the Lyceum took the step that would change its destiny. It finally altered its long-standing men-only policy and allowed women to become full-fledged members. Persistent efforts by the women members slowly produced improvements in the operation of the organization and turned it into a public facility. In 1895 the Lyceum began issuing book checks for $3 per year to adult Houstonians regardless of Lyceum membership. A year later, it made the library available to local high school students. Determined to improve the library facilities and to grow the book collection, the Lyceum finally convinced City Council that a public library was an essential ingredient for a progressive city and that it was worthy of public funding. In 1899, City Council appropriated $2,400 annually to maintain a free library.

Although this was an important step, it did not provide a site or a permanent building. The efforts of Houston women's clubs were instrumental in finally achieving the building. Mrs. W. E. Kendall and Miss Mamie Gearing, members of the Woman's Club, wrote a letter to Andrew Carnegie, a wealthy Eastern industrialist who was making cash grants for library buildings in many towns and cities throughout the country at that time. On November 17, 1899, the delighted members of the Woman's Club announced that Carnegie had agreed to give $50,000 to "erect a suitable building." Less than two months later, five women's organizations formed the City Federation of Women's Clubs to raise funds for a building site.

At that point, the Houston Lyceum transformed itself into the Houston Lyceum and Carnegie Library Association, selected a board of trustees, and initiated a campaign to solicit funds. Donations from private citizens, businesses, and City Federation clubs soon raised $7,880. With this sum, the city purchased a site at the corner of McKinney Avenue and Travis Street from the Presbyterian Church.

In December 1901, the city let a contract to the Martin and Moodie Company for the construction of a two-story Italian Renaissance-style building, and cornerstone ceremonies took place six months later. Mrs. Kendall set the first brick with a silver trowel. As work continued on the building, it became apparent that funds beyond the Carnegie gift were necessary to fireproof the structure, and the city allocated $10,000 more to complete and furnish the building.

While the building was under construction, the Library Association sought a Librarian. It found Julia Bedford Ideson in the new degree program in Library Science, instituted at the University of Texas in Austin in 1902. The Houston Lyceum and Carnegie Library Association tapped her for the job as Librarian, and by October 1903, Ideson began preparing for the opening of the facility. She would pro-actively strengthen and grow the Houston Public Library system over the next forty-two years.

On March 2, 1904, the Houston Lyceum and Carnegie Library formally opened to the public. The community had watched the construction of the building with great interest, and hundreds of Houstonians streamed through the doors to admire it. Henry H. Dickson, president of the Library Association's board, presented the building and its contents to Mayor O. T. Holt who replied, "In behalf of Houston and her citizens, I accept this building and may it ever be referred to with pride by all who may come into contact with it and those who fostered it." A telegram sent to Andrew Carnegie immediately after the formal reception expressed the city's appreciation for his gift and indicated that the library opened with fourteen thousand volumes.

Over the next decade Houston's growth challenged the downtown library's ability to serve the entire city. In response, Librarian Julia Ideson created extension services at public locations throughout the city. The first delivery station was opened at a drug store on the Liberty Road, where fifty books were placed for a period of six weeks and then exchanged for new ones. When this proved inadequate, the library entered into a cooperative venture to provide services for public schools without libraries. By 1916 stations were located in fourteen schools, a Boy Scout camp, two factories, and a church. In 1920 official library branches were established on the north side of the city in temporary buildings on school campuses, one at North Side Junior High School and the other at Heights High School.

During these years, Ideson initiated two campaigns to strengthen the library system. Realizing that the system required a broader funding basis in order to grow with the city, she launched a campaign for a municipal ordinance earmarking a percentage of city taxes for library purposes. The library board, civic groups, and local newspapers supported Ideson's proposal, and it was approved in a city referendum in 1921. At the same time, Ideson argued that the city had outgrown the 1904 structure. The city agreed and held a bond election in which the voters approved spending $200,000 for a new facility.

The city sold the property at the corner of Travis and McKinney back to the Presbyterian Church and used the $100,000 proceeds for two branch libraries, one on the north side and one in the Heights. The North Side branch replaced the building on the campus of North Side Junior High School in 1925. It was named Carnegie, since in 1921 the library system had officially been named Houston Public Library. The Heights branch opened in 1926, replacing the temporary building on the grounds of Heights High School.

In 1921, the Houston Public Library assumed control of the Colored Carnegie Library. The Colored Carnegie Library Association had established this library in 1913 with a grant from Andrew Carnegie. The Association operated it independently until it became a branch of the Houston Public Library.

Plans for a new central building began in earnest in 1922. After much consideration, the firm of Cram and Ferguson of Boston was chosen to design the building, along with two local associates, architects William Ward Watkin (who was also head of the Architecture Department at Rice Institute) and Louis A. Glover. They designed an L-shaped building, including a central register surrounded by east, west, and rear wings and an ell. When it became apparent that the bond issue passed earlier would not supply sufficient funds, the city postponed building the rear wing. Voters approved an additional $300,000 in bonds, and construction began on the remaining four units of the building.

The new building occupied the entire block facing Martha Hermann Memorial Square, bounded by McKinney and Lamar Avenues and Smith and Brazos Streets. Dedication ceremonies took place in Martha Hermann Memorial Square on the evening of October 18, 1926. The program featured Mayor Oscar F. Holcombe; architect William Ward Watkin; Mrs. A. K. Newby, president of the City Federation of Women's Clubs; Librarian Julia Ideson; and Rice Institute President Edgar Odell Lovett, who gave the principal address. A crowd estimated at 3,000 attended the dedication and then toured the handsome building, an obvious source of pride to Houstonians.

As the Houston Public Library resumed operations the next day, its collections numbered 110,878—a tremendous increase over the fourteen thousand volumes it had started with twenty-two years earlier. The staff had grown to thirty-five people. Along with the three branches—Carnegie, Heights, and Colored Carnegie—the system also maintained six stations—Harrisburg, West End, Park Place, Gable Street Settlement House, Council House, and Foley Brothers—as well as libraries in sixteen public schools. The library staff was acutely aware that the city was growing and that library services had to keep pace with that growth.

The 1930s brought both growth and decline to the library. In response to the financial difficulties of the Great Depression, the city reduced the library's budget and continued to postpone the long-awaited construction of the rear wing. However, government-funded agencies, such as the Reconstruction Finance Corporation, the Public Works Administration, and the Civil Works Administration provided physical improvements and clerical assistance to all of the library properties. The Public Works Art Project funded work by local artists on several murals and lunettes installed in the Central Building.

The library offered its services to a community in need. Library buildings were used as nutrition centers and as locations for conducting housing surveys. The library cooperated with the government's recovery program by supplying books to transient shelters and settlement houses. In spite of hard economic times, the collections grew by approximately fifteen thousand volumes each year, and circulation continued to climb in every area except the children's department.

Getting books to children became a particular challenge since families found it difficult to come downtown, and their homes were not always convenient to the three existing branches. To address this need, the library created a Traveling Branch in 1938. By visiting twenty-two neighborhoods every two weeks, the bookmobile reached thousands of new readers. In 1939, the system created a fourth full branch by building a permanent facility for the Park Place station.

The state of Texas observed its Centennial in 1936, and the Houston Public Library furnished resources to assist in telling the story of Texas' first one hundred years. The library had established a Historical Room in 1931, and during the Centennial it added many materials, especially those of a genealogical nature. Lists of books on Texas history were distributed to the schools; historical exhibits were installed throughout the year; and librarians compiled multiple scrapbooks, covering all aspects of Texas life, to furnish reference materials for researchers.

The 1940 census disclosed that Houston had become the twenty-first largest city in the United States. World War II and the years that followed brought more growth to the city, which in turn placed greater demands on the Houston Public Library. In spite of the fact that the city expended only twenty-three cents per capita on its library department (a very low figure, according to the American Library Association's standards at the time), Julia Ideson and her staff continued to serve the public. The library provided books on business and technology, especially geology, as war-related industries grew. The global war created demand for books about other countries and information about the different branches of the armed services. In 1942 the library conducted a Victory Book Drive in which the Red Cross collected twenty thousand books and the library distributed them to the troops. The single most requested book during these years was *Mein Kampf.* Patrons would say, "I want to know what Hitler's plan is for America."

The library survived the war years, increasing its annual circulation to 600,000 and adding another branch, West End. However, the library and the city experienced a tremendous loss when Julia Ideson died in July 1945. In one of her last annual reports, Ideson stated the vision that motivated her leadership in developing the library as an essential and dynamic part of city life:

> Demands for library service grow with the increasing complexity of
> life. Those who believe that modern improvements like radio and moving
> pictures will replace books and reading take a superficial view of the vital
> part books must play in man's endeavor. Modern inventions may compete
> for entertainment and even for instruction, but for accessible information on
> what man has thought and done, and an understanding of what man has hoped
> and dreamed—for the basis from which the future may be chartered—only the
> substantial qualities of the printed record will serve.

Her forty-two years of leadership established a strong basis for the library to continue to serve as a beacon in the community.

Martha Schnitzer, who had served as Assistant Librarian since 1908, was named Acting Librarian and, in 1948, became Librarian—a position she held for one year before retiring. Upon Miss Schnitzer's retirement, Harriet Dickson, Children's Librarian since 1924, was named to replace her. Miss Dickson (soon to become Mrs. Reynolds) would remain at the helm seventeen years and would oversee unprecedented growth of both the city and the library system. Under her directorship, branches were added, another bookmobile was placed in service, and three long-awaited book stacks were built in the Central Building. The Central Building was renamed for Julia Ideson in 1951.

The Houston Public Library expanded its work in the community by participating in such projects as Operation Head Start, the Houston Literacy Council, and Talent Preservation, a Houston Independent School District program designed to decrease teenage dropouts. As a result of these cooperative ventures, students of all ages used the libraries in ever-increasing numbers. Thirteen thousand library cards issued in March 1963 set a new record. However, it was difficult to keep up with the demands placed on the library system by Houston's more than one million residents spread out over 359 square miles. It was apparent that more branch libraries were needed and that the Julia Ideson Building was no longer adequate to serve as the system's central facility.

Harriet Dickson Reynolds's successor, David M. Henington, would oversee the construction of a new central library, new branch libraries, and the creation of regional libraries. Named the new director in 1967, Henington immediately initiated plans for a new building downtown, as well as expansion of the branches. In January 1970 Houstonians approved a $10.5 million library capital improvement proposal that included $9.5 million for a central library and $1 million for developing branch libraries. The city commissioned the firm of S. I. Morris to design a new building next to the Ideson Building and across the street from Houston's City Hall. On January 18, 1976, the larger, modern facility opened to the public. The Ideson Building took on a new role as a research center housing the library's historical collections. Construction of new branches continued, with the system boasting twenty-two facilities by 1976.

During these years the Library enriched its collections. It added new resources, including a film library, specialized materials to aid minority business groups, an archival and research center, and a lending library of framed art reproductions. To broaden the scope of services within the community, the library implemented a Model City Neighborhood project to improve the quality of life for Houstonians across the city. In this project, branch libraries became the catalyst for groups working together for the general improvement of their neighborhood.

Houston Public Library celebrated its 75th anniversary by recording over one million patrons using the Central Library. At the same time more demands were placed on the branch libraries as the city's traffic problems increased and the cost of gasoline rose rapidly. By 1985 the system had thirty-one branches in service. With immigrant communities growing in Houston, the library enlarged collections of foreign language materials and provided courses in English-as-a-Second-Language. It met additional community needs by adding both materials and programs for the hearing-impaired and sign language classes for the general public.

The decade of the 1990s brought continued growth to the Houston Public Library. Major accomplishments included increasing the circulation of materials, installing the "WiseCat" CD-ROM catalog throughout the entire system, and providing an on-line public catalog. Branches, now numbering thirty-five, were divided into regional clusters to facilitate delivering complete library services closer to patrons' homes. In 1995, upon the retirement of David Henington, Assistant Director Barbara A. B. Gubbin became the fifth person to assume the reins of leadership.

Improved technology became a focal point of the library system as it moved toward the twenty-first century. All facilities added new information formats to their resource collections: e-books, e-journals, CD-ROMs, compact discs, and videos. A Gates Foundation grant created seven computer-training centers that provided free instruction to Houstonians of all ages.

In 1999—a century after Andrew Carnegie made his original gift to the city to establish a free library—a grant from the Carnegie Corporation of New York enabled the library to meet the needs of its changing community. The Corporation awarded the Houston Public Library a $500,000 grant to create Libros y Más, a series of programs to serve the city's Hispanic children and their families, the fastest growing segment of Houston's population. At the same time, the library developed collections in other languages, including Chinese and Vietnamese. Two projects sought to motivate Houstonians to explore the power of books and reading. The Power Card Challenge targeted juvenile readers. Highly successful, it resulted in 303,000 children receiving library cards. To encourage adult readers, the library, in conjunction with the *Houston Chronicle*, created a city-wide reading project, Books on the Bayou: Houston Reads Together. Each year a month-long series of reading activities, based on a selected book, are held across the city.

As the Houston Public Library enters its second century, it remains committed to empowering the personal and professional growth of every person in the city. Evolving from the Houston Lyceum's intent for young men to "improve" themselves, it has combined Julia Ideson's vision of providing for everyone a resource that offers "the basis from which the future may be chartered" with the power of online databases and community-based programs. In an ever-expanding city with an international population, the Library faces a challenging future.

100 STORIES

At the dawn of the twentieth century, Houston was a relatively small trade center with a population of 44,633. The automobile was not yet in common use, and streetcars carried residents to downtown offices, to Levy Bros. for shopping, or to West End Park for a ball game. The tallest building on the skyline was six stories, and boats still docked at the foot of Main Street. Yet town boosters could proudly declare that Houston was the largest railroad center south of St. Louis, the second-largest manufacturing center in Texas, and the second-largest city in bank clearings in the South. Two events that would stimulate the city's growth were just over the horizon: the discovery of oil and the opening of a deepwater port. While Houston leaders nurtured an environment favorable to commercial and industrial growth, some recognized the importance of developing cultural resources to support the life of the community. Members of the Houston Lyceum began to take action on the long-felt need for a permanent public library.

In 1897, the Houston Lyceum rented three rooms on the fourth floor of the Mason Building as its new headquarters. The Mason Building, constructed in 1894 at the northeast corner of Main Street and Rusk Avenue, was a center of commercial and civic activity in downtown Houston. Women members of the Lyceum had pressed for the move to Main Street, objecting that it was inappropriate for ladies to go unescorted to the previous Lyceum quarters in the Market House at Travis and Preston. The move to the Mason Building spurred activism by women's clubs. The Ladies' Reading Club funded the move and gave the Lyceum their magazine files and their own library of nearly 150 books. To help in building the book collection, the Ladies' Reading Club voted to add $5 worth of books to the shelves each month. In return for the support of the women's clubs, the Lyceum offered the headquarters for meetings of the Ladies' Reading Club and the Shakespeare Club. Although the Houston Lyceum enlarged its list of subscribers and expanded its collection of materials, financial problems persisted. Supporters of the library soon realized that public funding was crucial for keeping the Lyceum alive.

The Ladies' Reading Club, organized in 1885 as the city's first literary club for women, recognized that a public library was essential to the community and that it would require a municipal appropriation. Although the city fathers periodically promised to do something, they took no action. The ladies finally planned a demonstration to motivate them. On January 23, 1899, they gave a reception for city officials in the Lyceum rooms in the Mason Building, with their sparsely filled bookshelves. The Lyceum ladies fed their male guests chicken salad, hot biscuits, and coffee and entertained them with a program of music and recitations. Then they pointed to the bare bookshelves and reminded Mayor Samuel Brashear that he had promised to establish a public library. Mayor Brashear assured the gathering that his administration would "cheerfully" attend to that matter, and on March 13, the mayor and aldermen redeemed their pledges by appropriating $2,400 per year for the maintenance of a library. The Lyceum quarters provided a free public reading room for residents of the city.

According to their charter, the Woman's Club of Houston organized in 1893 "to create a solidarity of feeling among women on a basis of common interest." Their interest in education and the broadening of their knowledge of art, literature, and history motivated them to work to create a public library for Houston. A charter member of the Texas Federation of Women's Clubs, the Woman's Club supported the Federation's projects for training professional librarians, organizing traveling libraries, and establishing a Texas Library Commission. Challenged to create a public library in Houston, President Belle Kendall and Secretary Mamie Gearing penned a request to Andrew Carnegie for library funds. Carnegie, a wealthy Eastern industrialist, was at that time making cash grants for library buildings in cities and towns throughout the country. The Woman's Club hoped that Carnegie would honor their request since they knew that the city's appropriation of $2,400 annually was not sufficient to fund a building. Kendall and Gearing mailed their letter and waited.

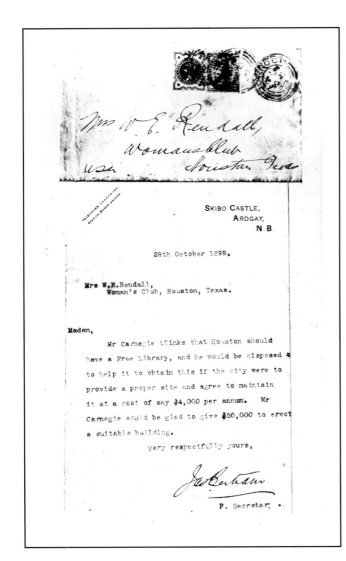

Andrew Carnegie replied to the appeal of the Woman's Club by promising the city $50,000 to erect a library building. Carnegie used his wealth to fund libraries because he was convinced that literacy would help working-class people succeed and that public libraries would promote good citizenship among newcomers to America. Over a period of two decades, Carnegie funded thirty-two public libraries in Texas. Some stipulations accompanied Carnegie's gift. He insisted that the library must always remain free to the public, and he required that the city donate a suitable building site near a park or the business district and that the city provide money totaling ten percent of the grant for continued upkeep. To comply with Carnegie's requirements, Houston's women's clubs—the Ladies' Reading Club, the Woman's Club, the Current Literature Club, the Shakespeare Club, and the Mansfield Dramatic Club—formed the City Federation of Women's Clubs to raise money for a site. They sponsored musicales, lectures, ice cream socials, and bazaars. Their efforts, combined with individual gifts, raised $7,880 which was used to purchase a lot near the business district, as Carnegie had stipulated.

While building plans were underway, the recently appointed Library Board began its search for a librarian. It contacted the University of Texas, which had instituted a course in library science in 1902, and discovered that Houstonian Julia Bedford Ideson was enrolled. Ideson had entered the university after graduating from Houston High School, with the intention of becoming a teacher. A lifelong love for books led her to enroll in the library science course. In Ideson's application for the Houston Public Library position, she confirmed that she had completed the required courses in library science and assured the Board that she was skilled in appropriate technologies: "…I use the typewriter, as you probably know, a requisite of the modern librarian." Letters of recommendation from university faculty described Ideson as "unusually energetic and intelligent," "agreeable and attractive," and "wide awake and ambitious." In October 1903 the Houston Lyceum and Carnegie Library Association hired Ideson, and she immediately began accessioning, classifying, and cataloguing materials to prepare for the opening of the new building. Over her forty-two year career, Julia Ideson became a leading figure within her profession and a community leader in Houston.

On March 2, 1904, the Houston Lyceum and Carnegie Library at the corner of Travis Street and McKinney Avenue was dedicated and opened to the public. A large crowd gathered to admire the Italian Renaissance building. Faced with grey pressed brick and trimmed with Bedford limestone, the structure featured a central dome, on which stood an angel with a scroll in hand. American eagles perched on the central pediment and the two corner pediments. The interior featured modern utilities, including gas and electric lighting and steam heating. Library trustees boasted that it was the only building of its size in the state in which all floors, ceilings, roof, and dome were totally fireproof. In his address for the dedication, Henry H. Dickson, president of the library association's Board of Trustees, welcomed the audience to "the inauguration of a means for the greater intellectual and literary advancement of the people of Houston." Dickson introduced the other members of the library board: J. R. Browne, W. H. Clute, C. P. Shearn, Mrs. W. E. Kendall, Mrs. H. F. Ring, Mrs. E. Raphael, T. M. Kennerly, and E. P Hamblen. President Dickson announced that the library had 10,000 volumes on the shelves, plus 4000 government documents. He invited those assembled to begin circulating the materials by checking out a book.

The library immediately became popular. The press noted that several hundred people entered the building each day. Patrons checked out and returned books at the delivery desk located on a raised platform in the rotunda, with a replica of Venus de Milo watching over. The Venus de Milo was a gift to the library from the Public School Art League, which originally purchased it to donate to a city school. When the School Board rejected the gift as inappropriate for a school, the League presented it to the library, where it has resided ever since. As might be expected from their participation in establishing the library, women were frequent patrons, and women's clubs met in a room in the library. To encourage male patrons, the library published an open letter that read:

> Caesar was quite a busy man, but found time to write a
> book. Don't you think you can find time to read one?
> Visit the library...It holds your books in trust for you.
> They are useless on the shelves.

Within three years of opening, over ten thousand Houstonians owned library cards.

When the Houston Lyceum and Carnegie Library opened, Julia Ideson had only one assistant, Ethel Jones. As the number of volumes grew and library patrons increased, the staff also expanded. By 1913 the staff totaled seven employees, including an assistant librarian, a children's librarian, several cataloguers, and a maintenance worker. The staff grew over the years as areas became more specialized, as circulation and services increased, and as the system added branches. Today the library has 582 employees.

On September 27, 1911, Dr. and Mrs. B. J. Covington hosted a dinner in their home honoring Booker T. Washington. Washington's visit lent support for a library for Houston's African-American community. E. O. Smith, principal of Hollywood School, had initiated plans for a library in 1907, when he organized the Negro Library and Lyceum Association. The original trustees of the Association were W. L. D. Johnson, R. G. Lockett, W. E. Miller, L.H. Spivey, and E. O. Smith. Later, J. B. Bell, Andy Parr, John M. Adkins, and Nat Q. Henderson joined the board. Julia Ideson helped to purchase and catalogue books, and the library station opened on May 5, 1909, at Colored High School on Frederick Street. As interest developed in expanding the station into a full-service branch library, Smith contacted Booker T. Washington. Washington's secretary, Emmett J. Scott, a native Houstonian, wrote to Andrew Carnegie, who had funded the first Houston Public Library building in 1904. Carnegie agreed to grant $15,000 if the trustees acquired a suitable building site and if the city government would maintain the library.

After receiving a favorable response for a grant from Andrew Carnegie, the Negro Library and Lyceum Association incorporated under the new name the Colored Carnegie Library Association. The Association purchased a lot at the corner of Frederick and Robin streets from the United Brothers of Friendship Lodge for $1,500, raising funds by running excursions, selling tags, and holding entertainments. William Sidney Pittman, the son-in-law of Booker T. Washington, received the commission to design the building. Pittman had previously worked on Carnegie-financed projects in Washington, D. C., where his office was located. His experience enabled him to employ design features that Carnegie now required of his grant recipients. Pittman designed a structure in classical style, with a buff-colored brick exterior and a green roof. It included an auditorium that seated 250 people. The Colored Carnegie Library was dedicated on April 11, 1913. The city relinquished control of the library station at Colored High School, and the trustees of the Colored Carnegie Library Association operated the Colored Carnegie Library independently until 1921, when it became a branch of the Houston Public Library. In 1962 the building was razed when Interstate Highway 45 was built through the Fourth Ward.

High school students visited the downtown library regularly, and the reference department became one of the busiest departments in the building. A report in 1917 listed these recent questions asked by patrons:

How many automobile licenses are issued in the United States?

What can be done to ripen bananas?

How many navy yards are in the United States and where are they located?

How are silos built?

How much petroleum is exported from Texas each year?

What is the character of the soil around Brownsville, Texas?

How do health conditions in Houston compare with those of other cities?

The library advertised that it had over a thousand reference books with answers to any questions. It encouraged patrons to telephone Preston 931 if they were too busy to visit the library in person.

In 1900 Mr. and Mrs. Norman S. Meldrum made a special gift to the library. They established a fund in memory of their daughter, Norma, who had died of scarlet fever in 1899 at the age of nine. The Norma Meldrum Children's Library Fund purchased books and periodicals for children from eight to fifteen years of age. The major portion of the Fund was set aside as a perpetual trust to be used for purchasing children's materials. When the Houston Lyceum and Carnegie Library opened in 1904, it named the children's room for Norma Meldrum. The library held story hours weekly and compiled and distributed reading lists for children. The Boy Scouts prepared a list each year entitled "Books that Boys Like Best." Among the most popular juvenile literature during these years was *The Wizard of Oz* by Frank Baum, Alice Hegan Rice's *Mrs. Wiggs of the Cabbage Patch*, and Rebecca of *Sunnybrook Farm* by Kate Douglas Wiggins. The Norma Meldrum Room continued to be a favorite place for children after it was relocated to the new Central Building in 1926.

Houston Public Library
Carnegie Building, Main entrance, February 1923.
Live oak trees on McKinney St. cut down Feb. 1923.

With Houston's phenomenal growth after 1910, the city quickly outgrew the Carnegie Library and made plans to construct a new facility. In 1921 the Carnegie Library changed its name to the Houston Public Library, and the Library Board was in the process of seeking a new site and designing a new building. This photograph, taken in 1923, shows the Carnegie Building hemmed in on its lot next to the Presbyterian Church, with construction under way to widen McKinney Avenue. The oak trees lining the street were removed soon afterwards. In June 1923 the library sold this property back to the Presbyterian Church, receiving $100,000 for the lot and the building. Real estate prices escalated over the next two decades and, in 1945, the half block containing the church and the former library brought the highest price ever paid for land in Houston—an astounding $2,000 per front inch, or $3,055,000 for the entire tract.

Houston Public Library
Administration Center
Fifth floor County Court House
Library Staff — Left to right
Anabel Norwood, Martha Schnitzer,
Julia Ideson, Janice Radetsky.
February 1925.

By 1920 workspace in the Carnegie Library was so limited that some members of the staff were forced to spend, according to librarian Julia Ideson, "four years of exile in foreign quarters." Those quarters were on the fifth floor of the Harris County Courthouse, where an overflow of library materials had been stored since 1911. In 1921, the county offered to let the library use this unfinished space while it completed plans for the new central library building. The library installed heating, lighting, wall partitions, and shelving in the 70' x 70' room. Martha Schnitzer, the Assistant Librarian, and Anabel Norwood, the Cataloguing Assistant, moved their offices into the courthouse. (They are seen here with Julia Ideson and Janice Radetsky.) The library also relocated its government documents to the courthouse. Houston had been named a depository for government records in 1884, and Ideson felt that it was important to retain them even though space was limited. Over time the staff shared space with the County Auditor, the County Law Library, the Tick Eradication Project, the Anti-Tuberculosis League, and the Veterans of Foreign Wars. The librarians were greatly relieved to relinquish the courthouse space and end their exile in 1925, when they moved the library materials to the new Central Building.

Houston Heights Branch 20th St.
Houston Public Library
Constructed in 1921 Cost 1731.31
Heights Senior High School at left.
Feb. 1922

Houston Public Library started a branch library in the Houston Heights in cooperation with a committee from the Parent Teacher Association of Heights High School. Mr. W. P. Waltrip, Heights principal, offered the use of a classroom, which was outfitted with shelving and furniture. The facility opened on March 1, 1921, with one thousand volumes. Four months later, a similar branch opened on Houston's north side in a room at North Side Junior High School. In the fall, crowded conditions made it impossible to use the library facilities in the schools. With permission from the School Board, the Houston Public Library erected temporary buildings on the campuses of Heights High School on E. 20th Avenue and of North Side Junior High School on Noble Street. The two buildings were identical, equipped with a small office, built-in shelving, a lavatory, and heaters. They remained in use until 1925, when permanent structures were completed for each branch, and the library sold the temporary buildings to the Houston Independent School District for $400 each. The sale in 1923 of the library property at Travis and McKinney funded the construction of the permanent facilities.

A wooded site on Henry Street became the location of the north side branch, which was renamed to honor Andrew Carnegie. City architect W. A. Dowdy designed a red brick building described as being reminiscent of Monticello in Virginia. Carnegie Branch Library opened on November 10, 1925 and served for fifty-five years. In 1980, it was razed and replaced by a new facility

with a unique mission. The Houston Public Library, the Houston Independent School District (HISD), and the Houston Community College System cooperated in a joint venture to establish an educational center. The center served as a community library, as school libraries for HISD's John Marshall Middle School and Jefferson Davis High School, and as a branch campus for Houston Community College. Ray Bailey Architects designed a contemporary building with angled glass walls facing the schools, and the classical columns from the original Carnegie building were placed in a park-like setting nearby. The new building was dedicated on December 5, 1982. The Carnegie Branch Library not only serves large numbers of students, but it also provides computer classes, English-as-a-Second-Language classes, income tax assistance, children's story time, and the After School Programs Inspire Reading Enrichment (ASPIRE) program for the community.

The Heights Branch Library opened on March 18, 1926, after being in temporary quarters for four years. The Italian Renaissance building, designed by J. M. Glover, quickly became a popular destination on Heights Boulevard. Many individuals and organizations made the library grounds a neighborhood attraction by providing landscaping, such as a large stone birdbath, a variety of trees and plantings, a formal garden surrounded by a wrought iron fence, and a memorial fountain. Jimmie May Hicks became a legend in the community by serving as head librarian for thirty-three years. In the late 1970s the Heights branch closed to construct an addition. Just after reopening, the building was listed on the National Register of Historic Places. The Heights Branch continues to serve many longtime residents alongside newcomers to the Heights. It offers an extensive collection of materials on the history of the Heights, which was Houston's first suburban development. The community looks forward to annual events such as the library's Christmas Open House and a book sale. The branch maintains a close relationship with the Houston Heights Association, Rotary Club of Houston Heights, Fraternal Order of Eagles, and the local chapter of the American Association of Retired Persons.

In 1907 a group of Houston women organized the Houston Settlement Association to address the needs of the many immigrant families located in the Second Ward. To offer services to these families, the Association opened Rusk Settlement House in the former Settegast home on Maple and Gable streets. In 1908 the Houston Public Library became a partner of the Settlement Association by establishing a library station at the settlement. When Rusk School was built nearby, the library extended its services there since few public schools at that time maintained libraries in their buildings. The children at Rusk School eagerly awaited the arrival of the librarians each week. The library reported in 1928 that the Rusk library had received 138 books, an English-Spanish dictionary, a few adult books in the Spanish language, and a subscription to *St. Nicholas* magazine. Even after individual schools opened their own libraries, the practice of bringing books to teachers in schools continued in a program called Teacher's Table.

The 1920s were dynamic years for Houston. In the Municipal Book of 1928, city leaders boasted about "the spirit of an awakening city, throbbing with new life." New neighborhoods seemed to spring up almost daily. Memorial Park added to the city's green space. The Houston Zoo and Miller Theater increased attractions at Hermann Park. The Museum of Fine Arts opened nearby as the first municipal art museum in Texas. Educational opportunities expanded with the opening of Houston Junior College (later, the University of Houston) and Houston Colored Junior College (later, Texas Southern University). Construction of the Niels Esperson Building and the thirty-six story Gulf Building, the tallest skyscraper in Texas, dramatically altered Houston's skyline. Numerous banks sprang up on lower Main Street. Elaborate movie palaces entertained fans of the silver screen. Ninety miles of streetcar track stretching in all directions supported this explosive growth, and the inauguration of airmail service sped up connections in and out of the city. By the end of the decade, Houston had become the largest city in Texas, with a population approaching 300,000. In the midst of this explosive growth, the Houston Public Library entered its third decade and planned for the future.

Houston Public Library
Bagby block, Lamar front (East) Feb. 1923.

When the library board of trustees determined in 1920 to replace the Carnegie Library, they considered several downtown properties before selecting a site three blocks west of the Carnegie building. The block bounded by McKinney and Lamar Avenues and Smith and Brazos Streets had held the residence of Thomas Bagby, a commission merchant and an incorporator of the first Houston Lyceum in 1848. The property faced Martha Hermann Memorial Square, a park donated to the city by philanthropist George Hermann in 1913. City Council approved the purchase of the Bagby property on September 22, 1922, and finalized the sale for $92,500 the following month. The site contained several trees dating back to the Bagbys' occupancy of the site. According to legend, Sam Houston planted an oak on the property when he visited his friend, Thomas Bagby. Although that tree no longer exists, the two large oak trees in front of the building are thought to have grown from a seedling and an acorn from Sam Houston's planting.

HOUSTON CARNEGIE LIBRARY.
DON HALL, CONT'R.
12-1ST-1924.

SCHLUETER
HOUSTON
TEX

The library board of trustees commissioned the Boston architectural firm of Cram and Ferguson to design the new library building. Ralph Adams Cram was nationally known for his designs for the United States Military Academy, Princeton University, and New York's Cathedral of St. John the Divine. Houstonians knew him as the master planner for Rice Institute, completed fifteen years earlier. Two local architects, William Ward Watkin and Louis A. Glover, acted as associate architects, and the trustees assigned city architect W. A. Dowdy to assist with the project. Julia Ideson made a tour of libraries from St. Louis to Detroit and from Chicago to Boston to gather ideas for the structure. The architectural design took into account her highest priorities: natural light, cross ventilation, and flexible space. Construction began in June 1924, just days before a previously defeated referendum was re-submitted to the voters. This time the library bond proposition passed. By reducing the size of the original plan, the architects succeeded in completing the project in seventeen months at a cost of $500,000.

The architects designed the new Central Library building in Spanish Renaissance style for visual appeal and to evoke connections with the Spanish history of Texas and the colonial Southwest. Ralph Adams Cram called it "a style of exceeding beauty," and William Ward Watkin noted it was the "very style that explorers and priests had re-embodied in their missions of Spanish America." The exterior consisted of buff-colored brick and concrete, with carvings in limestone, graystone, and marble. The roof was red tile. Red quarry tiles, terrazzo, and the extravagantly carved and stenciled dark oak brought the Spanish Renaissance theme to the interior. Father Harris Masterson Jr., chairman of the building committee, suggested using regional iconography on the building. The front facade bears the shields of the six countries under which Texas has been governed and likenesses of the first Europeans to arrive in Texas. Above the east wing entrance is the face of French explorer Rene Robert Cavelier, Sieur de La Salle, the first European to explore Texas; and over the west wing portal, that of Fray Antonio Margil de Jesus, the first Spanish missionary to establish a school in Texas. The cornerstone has the arms of the Houston family, modified by Father Masterson to show an open book. The library used this representation as an insignia for many years.

The most magnificent space in the building was the central delivery hall, which occupied the rotunda on the second floor. This was one of the busiest places in the entire library. In the delivery hall patrons searched the card catalogue, checked out books, and used reference materials. Richly carved oak columns upholding ornate entablatures mark the entrance to the delivery hall. Columns of Vermont marble provide support for the gallery above. The central focus of the building is the towering rotunda, extending from the second floor up through the open third floor gallery to the elaborately coffered ceiling. There the clerestory windows bathe the entire space in light. Beauty is evident everywhere, in keeping with Julia Ideson's philosophy: "It is not enough to be functional; a library must offer delight to the eye."

The main reading room held open shelves containing thirty thousand volumes and gave access to thousands of additional books in the closed stacks. Here patrons found best-selling works of fiction—*An American Tragedy* by Theodore Dreiser or *So Big* by Edna Ferber—as well as books on art, literature, travel, and biography. Soon after the building opened, a library report declared: "Reading is no longer done only for pleasure, but business and professional men and women must keep up with the latest development of their particular work." Accordingly, the library added books on business and technology. The room's furnishings adhered to the building's architectural design. Oak reading tables reflected the design of Renaissance refectory tables, and Renaissance carvings crowned the open bookcases. This space is known today as The Texas Room, where researchers use the collections of the Texas and Local History Department, the Archives and Manuscripts Department, and the Special Collections Department.

The Reference Department became one of the most heavily used departments in the library. Individuals requested answers to such questions as "Who was involved in the Boston Tea Party?" or "Where can I pay my taxes?" Requests came from many difference sources. The city's street department requested a list of Texas heroes to use in naming new streets. Librarians compiled figures on Buffalo Bayou's deviations for the city's engineering department, and they prepared bibliographies for the Houston Open Forum lecture series. Businesses requested geological maps and soil surveys. The library kept a record of the number of questions submitted to the reference desk. A 1937 count showed 23,000 requests submitted to the main library, and the count rose steadily each year. By 1990 it had reached the astounding figure of 3,769,748 for the entire system. Louise Franklin, seen here, joined the Houston Public Library staff in 1921 after graduating from the University of Texas. She became Reference Librarian in 1926, a position she held until her retirement in 1963.

The library staff posed for a photograph on the steps of the new building just after it opened in 1926. They are: (1) Miss Julia Bartels, (2) Miss Dorothy Cotton, (3) Miss Anabel Norwood, (4) Mrs. Fannie Cubley, (5) Miss Julia Bishop Smith, (6) Miss Dorothy Dowlen, (7) Miss Eva Lee Morgan, (8) Cecil Keith, (9) Miss Marian Cumming, (10) Mrs. Winfred Dunaway, (11) Miss Genevieve Williams, (12) Miss Julia Ideson, (13) Miss Janie Ogilvie, (14) Miss Louise Franklin, (15) Miss Martha Schnitzer, (16) Miss Jimmie May Hicks, and (17) Graves Toland. A new profession emerged as the number of public libraries grew throughout the United States and universities established library science schools to train librarians for the new demand. Library employees frequently had lengthy tenures, as did many members of the Houston Public Library staff seen here.

In June 1928, the Democratic National Convention took place in Houston. It was the first time a convention of this size had ever been held in Houston, and the city extended a warm welcome to the 25,000 delegates arriving in town. Since the library was near the convention hall (seen in the upper right of the photograph), it decided to participate in the event. It ordered a large supply of books and pamphlets on national affairs and urged Houstonians to use the materials to become better informed on the issues of the day. The library building provided the meeting place for the convention's Platform and Resolutions Committee. Members of the library staff served on the reception committee for the convention's Hospitality House, a building across from the library where delegates could hear the proceedings over loudspeakers and have access to writing rooms, telephones, water fountains, and emergency medical care. In recognition of the library's assistance, the convention bound the Hospitality House guest book and presented it to the library. Supporting civic endeavors became an important function of the library.

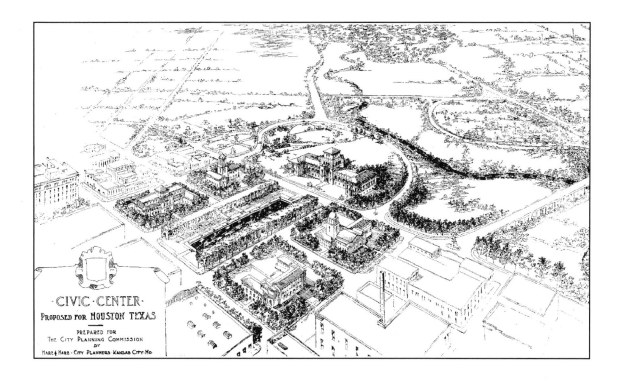

·CIVIC·CENTER·
Proposed for Houston Texas

Prepared for
The City Planning Commission
by
Hare & Hare - City Planners - Kansas City - Mo.

In the early twentieth century, Houston's municipal buildings included a market house and city hall, an auditorium, a library, and several fire stations. However, these structures were not part of a cohesive plan. In 1929 the City Planning Commission hired Hare and Hare, a Kansas City planning firm, to lay out a Civic Center. The Houston Public Library building was to be the cornerstone of the center, with all the buildings replicating the Spanish Renaissance styling of the library. Since much of the land around the library was in private hands and would have cost $1 million to purchase, City Council refused to approve the Commission's plan, and the idea of a Civic Center faded away. In 1937 the idea surfaced again when City Hall was relocated from its longtime site in Market Square to its present location. However, since architects designed the new City Hall in the Moderne style rather than the Spanish Renaissance, the idea of architecturally compatible buildings never materialized. When City Hall was completed in 1939, Martha Hermann Memorial Square was re-landscaped to include a reflecting pool. Today it provides an attractive view from the front door of the Julia Ideson Building.

The library received an extraordinary gift in 1931 when Annette Finnigan donated a collection of rare books and manuscripts that illustrated the evolution of bookmaking from early medieval times through the invention of printing. The collection, comprising sixty-five items, includes manuscripts printed and painted by hand, books produced during the early years of machine printing when hand illumination was still being done, Oriental scrolls, sheepskin rolls bearing religious messages, and a group of first edition books with their exceptional illustrations and fine bindings. The illuminated manuscripts are especially beautiful with their application of gold leaf, lapis lazuli, and ultramarine. A doctor of law diploma awarded to Vicentius de Dominis in 1764 exemplifies the skill required to produce an illuminated text. Annette

Finnigan was a leader in the woman suffrage movement in Texas and a philanthropist for the Museum of Fine Arts as well as for the Houston Public Library. When Finnigan died in 1940, she left an endowment of $25,000 to the Houston Public Library with the stipulation that the interest be used each year to purchase rare books and maps relating to the history of Texas, the Southwest, and Mexico.

John Ephraim Milsaps provided the basis for the Special Collections Department at the Houston Public Library. Motivated by the desire to provide his hometown library with the finest reference materials, Major Milsaps—native Houstonian, journalist, and Salvation Army officer—purchased books and official documents as he traveled around the world for the Salvation Army. He began sending materials back to Houston in 1903. Since he wished his gifts to be anonymous, the library identified them for many years only as the Circle M Collection. The collection contains 12,000 books and 3,000 pamphlets on subjects ranging from the Civil War to the domestic and foreign missions of the Salvation Army, plus seventy-four volumes of Milsaps' personal diaries. A large set of Bibles, representing almost every spoken language, includes Milsaps' personal Bible. Other rare items include first edition copies of classics like Melville's *Moby Dick*. Milsaps' accounts of his experiences in Houston in the early twentieth century record a significant period in the city's history. A portrait of John E. Milsaps, painted in 1932 by Grace Spaulding John, hangs in the Special Collections Department.

During the economic depression of the 1930s, one of the New Deal federal programs created work for artists. The Public Works Art Project put artists to work producing art for public buildings. It sponsored several works by local artists for the Julia Ideson Building. Ruth Pershing Ulher, longtime Curator of Education for the Museum of Fine Arts, Houston painted the mural seen here, *The First Subscription Committee, 1854*. It is a scene of Houston Lyceum supporters soliciting funds from a family, generally identified as the Thomas Bagby family. Angela McDonnell created a series of three murals — *Avila*, *La Rábida*, and *Toledo* — to represent the Hispanic heritage of Texas. Emma Richardson Cherry, Houston's first professional female artist, painted renderings of four historic structures: the Republic of Texas Capitol and the President's House (both located in Houston in 1837) and the homes of Jefferson Davis and Robert E. Lee. Cherry painted these depictions on canvas to be mounted on the walls of the library's Delivery Hall. The library's works remain the largest collection of depression-era art in the city.

Periodicals were an important part of the library from the time it opened in 1904, but they did not have their own space until the new building opened in 1926. A 1926 report declared that the new Periodical Room maintained a "splendid attendance" and a "full house." The report noted an increased interest in financial and geological publications and in French magazines, in addition to the constant demand for the standard popular magazines. The library enhanced the newspaper collection by acquiring back issues of early newspapers, dating to the 1836 issues of *The Telegraph and Texas Register.* These newspapers were considered so valuable that the library arranged storage at the University of Texas until it could provide fireproof housing for them in Houston. Patrons not only read current newspapers, but they frequently consulted older issues. A library visitor is seen here reading a bound newspaper in 1937. The library began microfilming the older papers in 1940 to prevent deterioration from handling. At the time when the Periodical Room sought larger quarters in the Auditorium of the Central Building, the library reported that it subscribed to 59 newspapers and to 697 periodicals.

The Traveling Branch, or Bookmobile, made its debut on September 27, 1938. Before it began making rounds, the library placed it on exhibit around the city. While it was parked downtown, newsboys called attention to it by shouting: "Extra! Hitler walks out on conference. Extra! Have you seen the new library?" The Traveling Branch scheduled visits to twenty-two neighborhoods every two weeks. It stocked approximately eighteen hundred books, and on a busy day half of those circulated. In addition to the demand for children's books and adult fiction, readers requested materials on subjects from slimming exercises to performing rope tricks. A second Traveling Branch was added in 1949 and a third one in 1960. One appreciative patron commented that the Traveling Branch was as "convenient as the corner drugstore and as friendly as one's own club." The demand was so heavy for books that the library posted a reserve list. Patrons waited patiently for books like *To Kill a Mockingbird* by Harper Lee and Thomas Wolfe's classic, *Look Homeward Angel*. The Traveling Branches ceased to operate in 1985 as additional branch libraries were built throughout the city.

Summer reading groups began as early as 1929. To encourage children to read during their school vacation, the library instituted a program that emphasized world friendship. Each "book traveler" kept a record of summer reading by placing stars on a map of the world. The reader's "trip" was complete after reading fifteen books. Another year the summer program was based on Texas history. Each library had a pictorial map of Texas, dotted with miniature log cabins. Each "reading pioneer" colored their cabin, log by log, to represent books read. The reader earned a diploma after completing twelve different kinds of books. Florence Bandy was the librarian when this Vacation Reading Club met at Colored Carnegie Library. Bandy had formerly been an assistant at the branch. After receiving her degree in Library Science from Western Reserve University, she returned to the Houston Public Library staff. Librarian Bessie Osborne had guided the Colored Carnegie Library during its early years.

In 1911 the Galveston-Houston Electric Railway began operating and the Park Place subdivision was platted. When Park Place became a stop on the interurban line, the convenience of commuting helped the neighborhood grow. In 1918 several Park Place families decided to organize a library, operating initially in a home and later in the Park Place Elementary School. The library was part of the Harris County Library system until the city of Houston annexed Park Place. The Houston Public Library assumed management of the library at that time and moved its books to the former Park Place City Hall. In 1939, residents and a grant from the Public Works Administration provided funds to build a small two-room structure, which opened on July 17, 1939, as the Park Place Branch Library. Over the next fifty years the building was remodeled and enlarged, and in 1995 it was replaced by a new one designed by Farrell, Sundin + Partners, Architects. The library has always received strong support from the community, and the Park Place Civic Club and the Park Place Literary Club continue that tradition today. Park Place is currently one of the system's four regional libraries.

World War II had a profound effect on Houston's industry and people. The city's industrial base expanded to meet wartime demands. A petrochemical complex developed along the Houston Ship Channel to produce aviation gasoline and synthetic rubber. Shipyards and aircraft factories provided employment to thousands of Houstonians, including women entering the work force in large numbers for the first time. On Memorial Day in 1942, one thousand young men gathered on Main Street to volunteer for the Navy to replace men lost on the cruiser *Houston* two months earlier. Civilians joined the war effort in many ways. They volunteered for the American Red Cross, collected scrap iron, and sold war bonds. Rationing became a way of life, with stamp books for meat, sugar, coffee, shoes, rubber, and gasoline. The Houston Public Library also felt the impact of the war. Its work force, especially maintenance workers and pages, decreased as young men left to join the armed forces. At the same time, the library experienced an increase in circulation. In the years immediately following the war, rapid population growth overwhelmed both the city and the library.

Following Julia Ideson's death in 1945, Martha Schnitzer became Acting Librarian. Schnitzer had been a member of the Houston Public Library staff since 1908, serving as Assistant Librarian for most of those years. A native of Germany, she worked in the New York Public Library before coming to Houston to be the Assistant Librarian. Schnitzer led the Houston library during the post-World War II years of rapid change. During that time, Houston's population surged, placing a great strain on the staff of fifty-three and on the facilities—the main library, five branches in library buildings, three sub-branches, four stations, and the Traveling Branch. In May 1948 Schnitzer accepted the appointment as Librarian, but retired ten months later. Her career with the Houston Public Library spanned forty-two years. The staff paid this tribute to her when she retired: "Loyal, friendly, helpful, interested…a good librarian, a sterling character, and a warm friend."

In 1948, Houston was tagged "the fastest growing city in the country." Just six years later the Chamber of Commerce held a celebration to welcome the metropolitan area's millionth resident. By the end of the 1950s, Houston had the seventh highest population in the country and was expanding geographically. In annexing numerous outlying districts, Houston became second only to Los Angeles in area. This growth during the decade of the 1950s brought change to every facet of city life. Construction began on a freeway system that city leaders hoped would relieve traffic congestion. Television appeared on the scene, and the nation's first educational channel began broadcasting from Houston. The Texas Medical Center grew from two institutions to a complex of medical facilities, developing a reputation for revolutionary research. Houston Ballet and Houston Grand Opera made their debut on Houston stages. Even professional football entered the picture with the formation of the American Football League. The 1950s also brought changes in race relations throughout the United States, and the Houston Public Library was integrated in 1953. In the decades that followed, the library faced the challenge of serving a larger and more diverse public.

Following Martha Schnitzer's retirement, Harriet Dickson Reynolds became Acting Librarian and took the position of Librarian in May 1950. Reynolds had joined the Houston Public Library staff as Children's Librarian in 1924 after receiving a degree in Library Science from the University of Illinois. During her tenure as head of the library, she oversaw many changes in the structure and services of the Houston Public Library system. The library added eight branches to accommodate Houston's expanding geographic boundaries. In 1958, much to the relief of staff and patrons alike, library buildings were air-conditioned. Separate departments established for Fine Arts and Business Technology emphasized specialization of knowledge and materials. Business firms increasingly submitted requests to the Reference Department, which handled 140,000 callers in 1965. That same year 81,000 new patrons applied for a library card, and the library estimated that 10,000 persons used the library system each day. Funding presented an ever-present problem, but Reynolds reminded the public that President Kennedy had called for "reborn greatness" in the country. Harriet Dickson Reynolds claimed that, since books contain greatness and contribute to greatness, the library had a mandate to respond to Kennedy's challenge.

Claude Bell joined the staff of the Houston Public Library in 1926 as the building superintendent for the Central Library. He assumed a tremendous responsibility in caring for a building of such architectural splendor, housing hundreds of thousands of books, not to mention irreplaceable papers and rare artwork. Bell is shown here on his retirement in 1952, after doing his job well for twenty-six years. The story of one of Bell's co-workers, J. Frank Cramer, has become a legend told and retold for more than sixty years. Cramer was a custodian for the Houston Public Library for ten years. He lived with his dog, Petey, in the basement of the Central building. Cramer, as the library's security officer, walked the building late at night, with Petey usually accompanying him. Cramer also played his violin after the building closed at night, preferring songs like "The Blue Danube Waltz." Following Cramer's death in 1936, fellow employees began to report strange happenings in the building. Some said they could hear Petey's claws clicking across the tile floors. Others reported hearing a strange sound like violin music. Was Mr. Cramer's ghost keeping watch over the library?

Originally named the Central Park Branch, the Nena E. Stanaker Branch Library opened on May 25, 1950, on 69th St. in east Houston. It was the fulfillment of a dream of Nena E. Stanaker, an area resident and library advocate. Stanaker had earlier laid the foundation for library service in the neighborhood by organizing libraries at Franklin and Edison schools. The Central Park building was renamed for Stanaker in 1968 when the building was enlarged. In 1985 a need for larger quarters led to the construction of a new building, designed by Molina & Associates. At that time the library also received a new address, since 69th Street had been renamed in memory of local war hero S/Sgt. Macario Garcia. Since the patrons of Stanaker Branch are largely first and second generation Hispanics of Mexican origin, the library sponsors activities that reflect Hispanic culture. Each year the library patrons eagerly anticipate events celebrating El Día de Los Muertos, ¡Que Viva España!, and Hispanic Heritage and Power Card Month. Every June and July the library conducts its Summer Texas Reading Club, in which children receive prizes for reading and participate in cultural and educational programs.

As early as 1939 it was apparent that residents of the Denver Harbor area were eager for library services. The reports of the Houston Public Library's traveling bookmobile showed that its most active stop was on Lyons Avenue in Denver Harbor. However, the community did not receive a library until 1953, when various community groups formed the Denver Harbor Library Committee. The Denver Harbor Branch opened on Market Street on September 16, 1953. It was the first air-conditioned building in the Houston Public Library system. The 1953 building served the community well for two decades. In 1978 the branch relocated to Cliff Tuttle Park to a larger facility designed by W. Norris Moseley. Upon completion of the new building, the branch was renamed for banker Clifford Francis Tuttle, a leader in the Denver Harbor community who was known for his work with neighborhood youth in recreational activities. An important part of the new library was an adult learning center that provided tutoring for those working toward their high school diploma. Tuttle Branch Library was renovated in 2000.

During the post-World War II years, much of Houston's dramatic expansion occurred on the west side of the city. After a survey of population trends and a review of the bookmobile's circulation, Houston Public Library chose a site on Willowick Road near Westheimer for a branch to serve a large area, including River Oaks, Afton Oaks, and Tanglewood. The branch was named for Adele Briscoe Looscan, a Ladies' Reading Club member who had been instrumental in founding the Houston Public Library in 1904. Architect Harvin C. Moore designed a contemporary structure to include such innovative features as a porte-cochere and a covered book slot for returning books in inclement weather. It also had the first planned parking space of any library. The Looscan Branch Library opened on March 6, 1956. The library received its first gift from the City Federation of Women's Clubs, which Adele B. Looscan had helped to organize in 1900 for the purpose of raising funds for the first Houston public library. Community organizations, as well as neighborhood residents, have continued to provide support for building its collections. Fifty years later the Looscan branch is serving its third generation of patrons.

Alice M. Young, in her role as a member of the Houston Public Library Board, was a strong advocate for the expansion of library services to all parts of the city. After her death in 1953, Mayor Oscar Holcombe and Sterling Hogan donated land to the city for a branch library, stipulating that it be named for Alice Young. The architectural firm Golemon & Rolfe designed a contemporary structure to complement the style of the adjacent Palm Center. On October 7, 1957, the Alice M. Young Branch Library opened. In 1996 the building suffered water damage and was forced to close. Houston Community College provided space for a temporary mini-branch until the new library opened in Palm Center in 1999. The branch has concentrated on children's services from the beginning, continuing that practice with ASPIRE (After-School Programs Inspire Reading Enrichment) as a major component of its programming. Young's computers are heavily used each day as juvenile patrons complete homework assignments and adults conduct online job searches and prepare resumes. The Old Spanish Trail Community Partnership and the Houston Area Urban League are strong community supporters of the Young Branch.

Children's programming had always been a strong component of the library and often involved collaborations with other community organizations. As early as 1920, the library celebrated Book Week with storytelling, exhibits, and art contests. This week-long observance evolved into the Summer Reading Program. As an incentive to encourage children to read, the prize for those who completed the requisite number of books during the summer included an invitation to attend a play. The library collaborated with the University of Houston in staging the plays, one of the most memorable being *Peter Pan*. In another collaborative effort for children, the library participated with the Houston Junior League in airing a weekly radio show, featuring librarian Ann Hornak (seen here) as the Pirate Queen. The show began with Hornak creating a story line by reading a few sentences. The young listeners then completed the story and submitted written entries to the library. Each budding writer received a book from the Junior League. Ann Hornak joined the Houston Public Library staff as Children's Librarian in 1949 and became Assistant Director of the Houston Public Library in 1957. She remained in that position until her retirement in 1989.

The Central Library opened a historical reference room in 1931. The library had been collecting documents pertaining to Houston and Texas since 1926, when it agreed to cooperate with the Harris County Historical Society to preserve the history of the Houston area. Books, documents, and newspaper files proved valuable when a sculptor sought a likeness of Sam Houston or an attorney needed land records to settle a boundary dispute. The library gradually added genealogical materials to the Historical Room. The genealogy collection grew through donations by individuals and the records of local patriotic organizations. Adele Briscoe Looscan left a significant bequest in 1936 when she willed her personal library to the public library that she had helped to found. Looscan's collection consisted of 1,567 books, photographs, pamphlets, and periodicals documenting early Houston and Texas. Mary Lewis Ulmer, seen here, was named to head the Historical Room in 1955. Mrs. Ulmer, a nationally known genealogist, was the first manager of Clayton Library Center for Genealogical Research.

In 1958 William Lockhart Clayton and his wife, Susan Vaughan Clayton, deeded their Caroline Street home to the City of Houston to be used as a library. W. L. Clayton, a founder of Anderson, Clayton and Co., the world's largest cotton firm, was active in government affairs, and, as a member of the Truman administration, guided the implementation of the Marshall Plan following World War II. Eminent Houston architect Birdsall Briscoe designed the Clayton's home in the Georgian style in 1917. In 1968, following the deaths of Mr. and Mrs. Clayton, the Houston Public Library moved its genealogical collection into the former residence, which became known as Clayton House. Houston Public Library had been collecting genealogy materials since 1921 and had allocated space for them in the Central Library when it opened in 1926. Over the years, the collection outgrew its space, numbering 4,718 volumes by 1959. Although the Clayton Library Center for Genealogical Research was constructed adjacent to Clayton House in 1988, the older building continues to house more than five thousand volumes of family histories. The Clayton House received a Texas Historical Marker in 1989. (Photo of Will and Sue Clayton courtesy Susan Garwood, photography by Gittings Studio.)

The library has always welcomed opportunities to interact with community groups that focused on education. When the new Central Library opened in 1926, it offered its auditorium and club rooms to non-political groups. Records from that opening year reveal that 210 meetings took place at the library. They included lectures sponsored by the Open Forum, classes taught by the City Recreation Department, a botanical symposium, activities of the Outdoor Nature Club, and meetings of the City Federation of Women's Clubs. Groups representing the arts and literature met frequently in the auditorium and included the Houston Scribbler's Club, the Houston Symphony Orchestra Association, and the Tuesday Musical Club. Most groups used the space free of charge, but often reciprocated in other ways. The Scribblers' Club assisted in writing publicity for library events. The League of Women Voters is seen here in 1960 at a meeting in the Julia Ideson Building, which preceded an information-gathering tour of blighted areas in the city. This tradition of sharing its buildings is evident in the library today. Every branch library has associated groups, who find a welcoming home at their neighborhood library.

Over the years the Houston Public Library made many friends who gave both time and money to support the services and the resources of the library. On January 27, 1953, a citywide Friends organization formed at a meeting held at the Woman's Club Building. Eighty-eight charter members elected Frankie Allen as the first president of the group. Under the direction of its board, seen here at a meeting in 1962 at which Mrs. Winifred Ellis is presiding, the organization has worked to provide funding for library programs and to raise the library's visibility within the community. Through the years the Friends of the Public Library has provided money for major collections of art books, a film library, and a circulating collection of art reproductions. In support of library staff, it established a scholarship program to assist librarians in attaining a graduate degree. The Friends' largest fundraiser is an annual Book Sale, which sells thousands of books to eager Houston bibliophiles.

Oak Forest was one of the largest residential developments in the country following World War II. As the number of families in the neighborhood increased, Houston Public Library decided to place a branch library there. A site on West 43rd Street was chosen for the glass-fronted, tan brick building designed by the architectural firm, Golemon & Rolfe. The Oak Forest Branch Library opened on October 6, 1961. As part of its initial collection, the branch received the 500,000th volume placed in the Houston Public Library system. The facility included a large meeting room, which through the years has provided space for Scout troops, Garden Oaks Civic Club, Garden Oaks Community Network, Oak Forest Coupon Club, Garden Oaks Elementary School, Black Middle School, Waltrip High School, and home-schooled students. Oak Forest still serves many of its earliest patrons, who visit the library in their retirement years. At the same time the library's proximity to schools helps the branch maintain a high juvenile circulation. As a result, the library's programs range from an annual Easter Egg Hunt to AARP's Tax Assistance Program.

By 1960 the southwest area of Houston was being converted from farmland to residential neighborhoods. George B. Meyer Sr., the developer of Meyerland, gave land on West Bellfort for a branch library, which was named for him. The library broke ground on November 14, 1961, for a building designed by architect Charles S. Chan. The new facility featured specially designed furniture, including tables shaped like a cloverleaf or a half-moon. It opened on July 25, 1962, to serve Meyerland, Westbury, Willowbend, Maplewood, Fondren, and Bellaire. The Meyer Branch was instantly popular. Reports indicated that a book circulated every 9.4 seconds on opening day. Although Meyer was the first branch library to open with full shelves, almost immediately it had to limit customers to two books per visit because of the overwhelming demand. Meyer Branch Library served as one of Houston Public Library's Neighborhood Information Centers in the 1970s and the 1980s. A third generation of participants now anticipates the annual 4th of July Children's Parade.

In 1963 Lakewood Branch Library opened on a heavily wooded site adjacent to Lakewood Park in northeast Houston. The architect for the project, Joseph Krakower, used the magnificent forest setting to good advantage. Over the years Lakewood Branch has cooperated with many community organizations, including East Houston Civic Club, Settegast Heights Civic Club, the Houston Parks and Recreation After School Program, East Houston Intermediate School, day care centers, and neighborhood churches. The branch has focused on family programming, with an emphasis on the growing diversity of the community. Bilingual programs for Spanish-speaking patrons, computer classes for senior citizens, and Juneteenth celebrations are popular activities. In June 2001 the Lakewood branch experienced severe damage from Tropical Storm Allison. As a result, the library was closed for a year in order to repair the building and to replenish materials. It reopened with a grand celebration in June 2002.

On July 31, 1964, the Houston Public Library opened its twelfth branch library. The new facility, located in the Spring Branch community, was named for Elizabeth L. Ring, a leader in the efforts of the Ladies' Reading Club to establish a free public library at the turn of the twentieth century. At the time of its opening, Ring was one of the largest branches in the system. The Texas Gulf Coast Chapter of the National Society of Interior Design recognized the architectural firm of Hamilton Brown & Associates for the outstanding library-in-the-round design, a unique plan at the time and one considered most appropriate for a library named Ring. The community supported the library from the day it opened. Only three weeks after the library's opening, when it became apparent that eighty-eight per cent of the books had been circulated, the Spring Branch-Memorial Chamber of Commerce began raising funds for additional books. Through a door-to-door appeal, in a short time the Chamber succeeded in collecting $6,300. Ring branch provides a variety of programming for children, including the Summer Reading Program and regularly scheduled story times.

W. L. D. Johnson Sr. was a longtime teacher in the Houston public school system and a founder of the Colored Carnegie Library. When informed that a branch library was to be named for him, Johnson wrote, "It is most difficult to live a satisfying life without good books." The W. L. D. Johnson Sr. Branch Library opened on June 16, 1964, in the Sunnyside community of southeast Houston. An outstanding feature of the building was a mural, *Birth from the Sea,* painted by Dr. John Biggers, art professor at Texas Southern University. When Johnson died in 1971 at the age of 102, he bequeathed $10,000 to buy materials for the library bearing his name. The community outgrew the facility by 1996 and drew up plans for a larger building, which opened in 1999. The new Johnson Branch, designed by Ferro-Saylors, Inc., is four times larger than the original one and displays bright colors—green, red, orange—on its exterior. The library carefully preserved the Biggers mural from its original site and restored it as a prominent feature of the new building. Popular programs at Johnson are Storytime and Parent/Child Playgroup, but regular patrons also include adults and students of all ages.

When Sharpstown was developed in the 1950s, national publications hailed it as "a new experiment in our way of life." This totally planned community was to contain everything that residents could want or need. A library became a part of the community on August 18, 1965, when the M. E. Walter Branch Library opened. Walter, a former editor of the Houston Chronicle, had campaigned in his editorials for an improved library system. The building, designed by Harvin C. Moore, opened with 26,000 books on the shelves and publicized that it had reading material for every man, woman, and child in the community. In 2001 the facility closed for major renovations to the existing structure, providing additional space with a meeting room and a conference room. While this work was being done, a temporary mini-branch opened in space provided by City Councilman Mark Ellis in his District F office in the Sharpstown Shopping Center. During this time, the branch received the honor of a Texas Book Festival Award. Walter Branch Library reopened in January 2003 and continues to serve a multi-lingual, international community. (Photo of M. E. Walter ©*Houston Chronicle*)

In the mid-1960s Houston Public Library participated in two community programs to enhance the educational experiences of children and teenagers. Operation Head Start, a national program designed to help children achieve educational equality before entering school, became a major cooperative community project for the library. Preschool children, who were enrolled in the eleven Head Start Centers, made trips to the library to gain experience in using a library and to enjoy special story hours arranged for them. For many of these children this was their first visit to a library. During the eight-week program, busloads of children arrived at the Norma Meldrum Children's Room. Head Start groups also visited branch libraries, including Carnegie, Central Park, Denver Harbor, Heights, Johnson, Lakewood, Looscan, and Young. In order to address the needs of teenagers, the library worked with the Houston Independent School District in their Talent Preservation Program. Designed to prevent students from dropping out of school, the program focused on encouraging reading while improving reading skills. Librarians prepared talks on books, gave tours of libraries, and compiled special collections of books for teens.

When Harriet Dickson Reynolds retired in 1967, the library invited David M. Henington, assistant director of the Dallas Public Library, to assume the leadership of the Houston Public Library. It was a homecoming for Henington, who, as a teenager, had worked as a page in the Central Library. After receiving a Master of Science in Library Science at Columbia University, he had returned to Texas and worked in Dallas and as director of the Waco-McLennan County Public Library before coming back to Houston. Henington's first concern upon becoming director of the Houston Public Library was the crowded condition of the Central Library. He initiated plans for a new building, which was completed in 1976. Henington then directed the renovation of the Julia Ideson Building. Henington's keen interest in providing research facilities led to establishing a genealogical research library in 1968 and the Houston Metropolitan Research Center in 1975. During his twenty-seven year tenure, he also opened twenty-two branches. The library entered the technological age under Henington. Computers became standard equipment in every library building as electronic technologies became the key to accessing information.

When the Houston Public Library purchased a one-acre site in far west Houston in 1966, Houstonians quipped that "the library will be built halfway between Houston and San Antonio." At that time the Memorial Drive area was only sparsely developed. However, when the new facility opened on January 21, 1969, its neighborhood was growing rapidly. The branch library, designed by the Alexander, Walton & Hatteberg architectural firm, was named for Belle Sherman Kendall, the Woman's Club member who wrote the letter in 1899 to Andrew Carnegie soliciting funds for a public library for Houston. Kendall's collections grew through the years as the staff developed relationships with a variety of neighborhood groups. Quilters, book clubs, and civic organizations have used Kendall as a meeting place, while supporting the library by contributing funds for special purchases. The branch's world language collection includes a large selection of Japanese books donated by the Japan International Trade Association, as well as books in Spanish, Chinese, and Vietnamese.

The dedication ceremonies for the William A. Vinson Branch Library were held on July 29, 1969. The facility, located on West Fuqua, was built to serve a growing section of southwest Houston. Its namesake, a founder of the Vinson and Elkins law firm, served as president of the Houston Library Board for twenty-five years. Architect Clovis Heimsath employed innovative design features in the building, including curved lines throughout the red brick building, with skylights and custom designed circulation desk, reference tables, and display case. Vinson enjoyed much popularity when it opened and continues to maintain a strong relationship with civic clubs and schools in the area. The branch regularly hosts an investment club, an adult reading club, cooperative projects with Madison High School, and Cinco de Mayo celebrations. Children's programming is a high priority at Vinson, with a consistently high registration in the Summer Reading Program.

Prominent businesswoman Nettie Moody gave to the city the forested property on Irvington Boulevard in northeast Houston, where the Nettie Moody Branch Library opened on January 2, 1969. Chan, Knostman, & Webster designed the streamlined library building for maximum flexibility and minimum maintenance. It included a children's area designed to be particularly appealing with its child-size furniture and a "happy" gold rug for floor activities. Moody has always served a wide range of patrons. Students at nearby Sam Houston High School frequently use the library's resources. The library features special programming for seniors and a Young Adult Collection for teenage readers, and the library staff has collaborated with Arte Publico Press on special exhibits. Community organizations actively involved with Moody Branch are East Sunnyside Civic Club, Hawthorne Place Civic Club, North Freeway Leader, Northline Park Community Storefront, and neighborhood schools. (Photo of Nettie Moody courtesy of Dan Moody III)

Houston rode a crest of prosperity and progress in the decade of the 1970s. The Port of Houston led the nation in foreign tonnage. Houston became the first city in the United States to issue more than $1 billion in building permits in one year. Nationally known architects created a stunning new downtown skyline. Texas continued to lead the nation in oil and gas production. Suburban subdivisions spread far beyond the central city. Houston, known in the past by names like Magnolia City and Bayou City, now assumed the label Space City for its role in the nation's space program. In fact, the entire world heard "Houston" as the first word spoken when men landed on the moon. The Houston Public Library shared the wave of progress in the 1970s. The city constructed a new central library and opened eleven new branch libraries. The number of patrons increased each year. By the end of the decade, for the first time ever, a million persons came through the doors of the Central Library in a year's time.

To broaden the scope of services offered to the community, the Houston Public Library implemented a Model City Neighborhood Project in 1970. The Project, which operated through film showings, adult education classes, and heritage clubs, sought to improve the lives of residents within fourteen square miles of the neighborhoods chosen to be models. Each neighborhood library in the Project concentrated on building collections in audio-visual materials, paperback books, magazines, and newspapers, which could be used with participants. Since some of these neighborhoods had a large Hispanic population, library staff enrolled in classes where they studied the Spanish language and culture. The Neighborhood Information Center Program was an outgrowth of the Model City Neighborhood Project. The Neighborhood Information Center Program gathered information on the needs of a neighborhood through surveys and neighborhood canvassing. Through the Neighborhood Information Center Program and the Model City Neighborhood Project, the branch library became the neighborhood center and served as a catalyst for establishing councils that worked for the general improvement of the neighborhood.

On March 23, 1970, a new branch library opened on a one-acre site in the Almeda Shopping Center. The new facility was named for J. S. Bracewell, an attorney and civic leader, who served twenty-six years on the Houston Library Board. The architectural firm of Neuhaus & Taylor designed a light brick building to blend with the Spanish architecture of the shopping center. J. S. Bracewell Branch Library was the first one in the system to have an audio-visual collection. It included tapes of classical, operatic and popular music, as well as literary recordings. Slides, filmstrips, and 8mm films were also available. Another innovative addition was a collection of paperback books for both adults and juveniles. Shortly after opening, Bracewell Branch, to the delight of neighborhood children, sponsored a pet show with over one hundred entries competing for most unusual, best groomed, and smartest pets. Bracewell provides materials for a loyal adult clientele, as well as activities for children, such as the Summer Reading Program and Pre-School Story Time. (Photo of J. S. Bracewell courtesy Elizabeth Bracewell)

The proposal to establish a library in Kashmere Gardens represented an important step in the expansion of the Houston Public Library system. The area had a potential patron base of 50,000 residents, and the branch could also serve as a "mother library" to smaller ones in Trinity Gardens and Denver Harbor. Don J. Tomasco & Associates designed a contemporary building featuring fluted columns on a raised podium and a bronze aluminum fascia. The Kashmere Gardens branch opened on November 16, 1971. In 1993, the branch added the name of Dr. Eva Alice McCrane to honor her distinguished thirty-year career with the Houston Independent School District. Although the branch closed for renovation in June 2001 in the wake of tropical storm Allison, it had served as a refuge for many local residents whose homes had flooded. A unique collection at McCrane-Kashmere Gardens Branch contains the photography of Earlie Hudnall Jr. The branch is also unique in claiming First Lady Laura Bush as a former staff librarian. (Photo of Eva Alice McCrane courtesy Charles McCrane)

Just one day after the McCrane-Kashmere Gardens Branch opened, the Houston Public Library opened the Arnold L. Hillendahl Branch in the Spring Branch community. The Hillendahl family had been an integral part of that area since its beginnings as a farming community in the 1830s. Architectural firm Pitts, Phelps & White designed a contemporary off-white brick structure with a Spanish influence. The completed facility, dedicated on November 17, 1971, was built to serve more than 25,000 residents within a twenty-five square mile area. At the dedication ceremony Mr. Hillendahl presented the library with a check for $500 to use in purchasing books. Friends of the Houston Public Library added another $500 to those funds. Hillendahl Branch Library is part of a multi-cultural community today, and its programming reflects that diversity. Timber Oaks Civic Association and Spring Branch  Civic Association are actively involved with the library. Although most of the libraries named for an individual have a portrait of that person in the building, Hillendahl has, perhaps, the most unusual one. In addition to a traditional portrait, there is a portrait of Arnold Hillendahl with his mule, Jock. (Photo of Arnold Hillendahl ©*Houston Chronicle*)

The fact that the Trinity Gardens neighborhood did not have a public library bothered Amanda Dixon, a librarian with the Houston Independent School District. In 1965 she organized a library that operated after school hours at Rosa Lee Easter Elementary School. In 1967 Mrs. Dixon's library moved into two rooms in the Christ Holy Sanctified Church on Hirsch Road. Seeking larger quarters for the book collection, Amanda Dixon continued to campaign for an official branch library. Her persistence resulted in a groundbreaking in January 1971 for a building designed and constructed by the Stran-Steel Corporation. Although Dixon died a month later, the library she had valiantly championed opened on October 9, 1971. Begun as a community effort, the library still works with organizations such as Trinity Gardens Civic Club and City Wide Beauty Club. Amanda Dixon loved books and frequently commented that she wanted to bring books and "the desire to soak up knowledge" to the young people in her community. The Amanda E. Dixon Branch Library is serving that purpose.

On June 2, 1974, Congresswoman Barbara Jordan made the key address at the dedication of the Lonnie E. Smith Branch Library. This presentation by the first African-American Texan elected to the U.S. Congress was a particularly appropriate celebration for the opening of the branch named for Lonnie E. Smith. Smith was the plaintiff in the landmark 1944 Supreme Court case *Smith v. Allwright*, which won African-Americans the right to vote in Texas primary elections. For the Lonnie E. Smith Branch, architect John Chase designed a contemporary brick building enhanced by expanses of tinted glass. The facility included a 120-seat meeting room. Groups that have been active at the Smith Branch include the Third Ward Community Cloth, S.H.A.P.E. Community Center, and San Jacinto Girl Scout Council. Since Smith Branch is located near Texas Southern University and the University of Houston, the library has built strong collections in reference materials and African-American studies. For younger students the annual Summer Reading Program is a highlight of the year.

In 1950 the grasslands just north of the Houston Ship Channel became the site of the Pleasantville subdivision, the first deed-restricted neighborhood for African-Americans in Houston. Although only one road led to it in the beginning, the community grew over the years as schools and parks were added in the area. In 1974 the Houston Public Library opened a branch library in Pleasantville. Architect W. Norris Moseley designed a building that provided attractive and comfortable surroundings. The Pleasantville Civic League, active in the community since its inception, has been a strong supporter of the library over the years. On June 9, 2001, the Pleasantville Branch suffered heavy damage from Tropical Storm Allison. Even though the library itself was flooded, it served as a temporary shelter for neighborhood residents trapped in their cars or driven from their homes. Staff and residents alike subsisted on little more than snack food all weekend. In the wake of the flood, the library closed for eight months for renovation and repair. It reopened on February 4, 2002.

Eleven branch libraries opened during the 1970s, a decade of rapid growth in Houston. The construction of new branches resulted from a survey authorized in 1969 by the Library Board and the City Planning Commission to study the needs of the library system and to plan an expansion program during this population surge. Three new branches opened in 1974 alone. One of these was built in southeast Houston and named for Lucile Yvonne Melcher, who, with her husband, Leroy Melcher, had given the land for the building. Lucile Melcher also established a fund for the on-going support of the children's collections at the Melcher Branch Library. Architect W. Norris Moseley designed the functional, brick structure. An innovative feature of the facility was a sliding glass wall separating the adult and juvenile areas, which could be opened to provide a large multi-purpose room for meetings and other planned activities. Ingrando Park Association is actively associated with the Lucile Yvonne Melcher Branch Library, which remains an integral part of its neighborhood.

The Julia Ideson Building had served its purpose for almost fifty years, but by the 1970s it could no longer contain the library's growing collections and expanded programming. The city determined to construct a new facility and chose the block just west of the Julia Ideson Building as its site. The property had been serving as a parking lot, but the location seemed ideal since it would enable the old and new buildings to form a library complex. Closing Brazos Street between McKinney Avenue and Lamar Street created an open plaza between the Julia Ideson Building and the new structure. Construction began in 1975. The firm of S. I. Morris Associates designed the building, with Eugene Aubry as the principal architect. They designed an octagonal building of granite, with a central core housing a vertical transport system, offices, and workspace for staff. An underground parking garage provides 150 sheltered spaces. Spanning eight floors (including two underground) and 334,000 square feet, the new structure was planned to meet the library's needs for the next two decades.

The library kicked off the nation's bicentennial celebration with a special event of its own. It dedicated the new Central Library on January 18, 1976, [with Mrs. A. T. Carleton, Library Board President, cutting the ribbon, assisted by Mayor Fred Hofheinz and former mayor Louie Welch.] Following the tradition of the 1904 and 1926 library openings, the assembled crowd toured the new building after the ceremony. Entering a three-story glass-walled lobby, visitors found themselves in a monumental light-filled interior. An architectural journal described it as "Houston's first successful outdoor civic space—magnetic, joyous, and alive." Color-coded walls identified different departments, and the deep red carpeting created a feeling of warmth in the large open spaces. After that first day, patrons returned in large numbers to use the library, especially enjoying the new Sunday afternoon hours. During its first year of operation, the Central Library circulated over 600,000 books and other materials. Besides its vast array of books, videos and DVDs, this facility houses federal government documents and a variety of special collections, including the Lurine Karon Greenberg Fine Arts Collection, which contains important works of architecture, art, and antiques. The telephone reference service is located here, and there is an Access Center, containing materials for the visually impaired. The library hosts classes from schools in the surrounding area on a regular basis, and periodically displays special exhibits.

Modern art and historic architecture merged in the new library complex. An anonymous donor offered *Geometric Mouse X*, a brightly painted steel sculpture, for placement on the open plaza between the Julia Ideson Building and the new Central Library. The abstract piece of art generated enormous controversy with the City Council, but they finally voted to accept it. The sculptor, Claes Oldenberg, explained that he used the mouse theme to inject irony and humor into the landscape. *Geometric Mouse X* was the first piece of public art installed in downtown. The library then began an extensive restoration of the vacated Julia Ideson Building. When the work was completed, the Houston Metropolitan Research Center (HMRC) moved into the building, where it remains housed today. The Julia Ideson Building was listed on the National Register of Historic Places in 1977 and received a Texas Historical Marker in January 2004. It also has been designated a City of Houston Historic Landmark. In 1989 the Central Library was renamed the Jesse H. Jones Building to recognize a generous gift from Houston Endowment, Inc. and to honor a man frequently referred to as "Mr. Houston" for his many contributions to the city. (Photo of Jesse H. Jones courtesy Houston Endowment, Inc.)

Rice University, Texas Southern University, the University of Houston, the Southwest Center for Urban Research, and the Houston Public Library joined in a venture in 1974 to establish a regional research center to preserve historic documents from Houston's history. They created the Houston Metropolitan Research Center (HMRC). In 1976 the Houston Public Library assumed sole responsibility for HMRC. The repository, housed in the Julia Ideson Building, contains archival materials on businesses, religious institutions, civic clubs, and other groups that have influenced Houston's development, as well as the papers of individuals who shaped the city's history. An Architectural Archives contains documents relating to Houston's built environment. The photograph collection includes more than three million images of Houston from its nineteenth century beginnings to the present. HMRC's Texas and Local History department has a vast collection of books, periodicals, government documents, and maps. The collection of maps includes this rare 1869 map, seen here being examined by Dr. Louis Marchiafava, HMRC archivist for twenty-five years. In 2003 a group of Houstonians formed the Friends of the Texas Room to support the activities of HMRC.

The first regional branch in the Houston Public Library system opened on October 20, 1975. It was named for J. Frank Jungman, an early developer on Houston's west side who played an important role in expanding Westheimer Road from a two-lane gravel road to a paved six-lane artery. Architects W. Irving Phillips and Robert Peterson matched the new role of the regional library with a new concept in building design. Rejecting the inward-facing, closed-box design typical of libraries, Phillips and Peterson produced an open design, with glass facades facing outward onto busy Westheimer Road. The Houston Public Library formed regional libraries to combine the convenience of a neighborhood branch library with many of the services of the Central Library. As a result, Jungman built a large collection of books in specialized areas such as petroleum, electronics, physics, mathematics, chemistry, and small business administration. Jungman has enjoyed a cooperative relationship over the years with Grady Middle School. It has also worked closely with the Gulfton-Bayland Park community in their Camp del Sol summer program and in the Bridge program that encourages parents and children to work together.

The Acres Homes community, named for its plentiful one-acre home sites, was developed in northwest Houston in the early 1940s. As the area grew, the library acquired property on West Montgomery Road, and the architectural firm of Haywood, Jordan, McCowan Inc. designed for the branch a light-filled building featuring natural materials. The program for the dedication on December 7, 1976 declared: "The love of books is contagious and spreads by each and every kind of encouragement." Acres Homes branch has offered that encouragement to patrons ranging in age from young children to retirees. Popular activities at the library have included the Summer Reading Program, Black History Month, and ASPIRE. Following a renovation, the library reopened to the public on May 24, 1999, including a Power Card Rally in its celebration. Acres Homes Chamber of Commerce, White Oak Terrace Civic Club, Garden City Civic Club, and Trinity Gardens Civic Club are actively involved with the library.

Fifth Ward Branch Library opened on October 10, 1977, on the city's north side. It was the first branch library located inside a City of Houston multi-service center and remains the only one in that kind of setting. Much of the library's programming involves staff interaction with the Head Start program housed in the center. Adult patrons are avid users of the library's audio-visual materials. For the past twenty years, Fifth Ward Branch Library has hosted a Black History Month program, accompanied by a dinner.

The Patricio Flores Branch Library traces its beginnings to 1943 when a reading room was opened at Ripley House Community Center. The library station grew from a collection of two thousand children's books to a much larger one that provided materials for adults, as well as for high school and college students. In 1982 Molina & Associates designed a building that was the first City of Houston facility to incorporate a solar air conditioning system. The 180 solar collectors used for both heating and cooling give the structure its unusual roof angle, which automatically influences its shape. The library, which opened on November 4, 1982, was named for the Most Reverend Patricio R. Flores, Archbishop of San Antonio. Flores was the first Mexican-American elevated to the hierarchy of the Roman Catholic Church in the United States. The Flores Branch receives active support from civic organizations and social service agencies in its East End neighborhood. Programming over the years has included Cinco de Mayo celebrations, Hispanic Heritage Month activities, and classes in the English language.

Houston Public Library named the Frank O. Mancuso Branch after the City Council member who represented District E in 1982, when the branch was planned for the southeast area. Architects Charles Chan and Philip Chang designed a contemporary brick building, with an auditorium and a conference room for community activities as well as for library programming. Upon its opening, an integral part of the library was the Neighborhood Information Center that assisted patrons in resolving everyday problems and referred them to community agencies for more serious ones. Mancuso Branch Library maintains a strong relationship with neighboring groups, including Andover/Southview/Fairlawn Civic Association, Bayou Oaks Civic Club, Garden Villas Civic Association, and Overbrook Civic Association. It conducts storytelling hours for children on a regular basis in cooperation with a near-by charter school, and it provides adult learning through the GED and English-as-a-Second-Language programs.

The Morris Frank Branch Library was dedicated on October 30, 1983, with these words: "We dedicate [this library] to the best of that which is human with the knowledge that unless we preserve the deeds and thoughts of humanity in books, we will never know the possibility of what that best can be." Named for Morris Frank, longtime Houston newspaper columnist, the library's distinctive building with its enameled porcelain exterior was designed by Barry Moore. In a neighborhood where residents speak Spanish, Vietnamese, Chinese, Hebrew, and Russian, the library building is an active community center, providing immunization clinics, income tax assistance, and computer classes. Book readings by popular authors and educational exhibits offer enriching experiences. Frank Branch collections include a Texana reference section established to celebrate the Texas Sesquicentennial in 1986. The branch also contains a large collection of memorabilia associated with Morris Frank's career.

In 1986 Houston observed the sesquicentennial of its founding. The city had grown in 150 years from a small settlement on a meandering bayou to become the fourth largest city in the nation. To commemorate the sesquicentennial, the Lone Star Chapter of the American Needlepoint Guild created a needlepoint tapestry entitled, *Houston Past and Present*. Ninety-six needlepointers worked for three years to complete it, and they estimated that the 8' x 8' tapestry contains two million stitches. The chapter presented the artwork to the City of Houston, which chose to place it in the Julia Ideson Building. Some of the squares reveal events from Houston's rich past; others point to the cultural, educational, and civic offerings in the city. One of the squares depicts the doorway of the Julia Ideson Building. The tapestry, capturing both the past and the present, portrays for visitors much information about Houston.

Originally named Dairy, Alief renamed itself after its postmistress, Alief Magee, in 1917. It retained its name when Houston annexed it in the 1970s. The Alief Branch Library opened on August 19, 1985, on a two-acre site in far southwest Houston. The White Budd Van Ness Partnership designed an exceptionally functional facility, including the latest in automated equipment. The building was enlarged in 1996 and renamed to honor David M. Henington, Director of the Houston Public Library from 1967 to 1995. A rededication ceremony was held on May 18, 1996. Henington-Alief Branch Library's diverse programming has included folklorico dancing classes for children, a Super Neighborhood Meeting hosted by the city's mayor, and a community news forum with a local television station. The branch also works closely with such neighborhood groups as the Chinese Community Culture Center, the Alief Independent School District, the Alief Noon Lions Club, and Alief Super Neighborhood. Henington-Alief Branch Library is one of four regional libraries in the Houston Public Library system.

The Everett D. Collier Branch Library was dedicated in ceremonies on September 28, 1985. Collier was a former editor and senior vice-president of the *Houston Chronicle.* The dedication ceremonies announced, "The Everett D. Collier Library is a fitting tribute to a man who was always an avid reader." Located near the Inwood Forest neighborhood in northwest Houston, the library's distinctive building by MRW Architects features a blue glazed exterior and a Texas tin roof. The branch houses a basic collection of approximately 50,000 volumes, magazines, phonograph records, cassette tapes, and computer software, and it is currently one of four regional libraries in the Houston Public Library system. Classes in English-as–a-Second-Language have been a focal point of adult programming since the branch opened. The library also provides GED classes, books to help the non-reading adult, and books in Spanish and Vietnamese. In addition to a well-attended Summer Reading Program, the branch also has an active ASPIRE program.

ASPIRE stands for After School Programs Inspire Reading Enrichment. The library instituted the ASPIRE program to provide young students with stimulating learning experiences in a library environment. Volunteers provide homework assistance and tutoring, as needed. Librarians introduce students to reference materials, the Internet, and other library resources as tools for learning. The students use these aids to prepare their school assignment, or they may choose to explore on their own. The library plans activities to enhance the learning experience, including poetry readings, guest speakers, musical performances, web-making sessions, and craft classes. The ASPIRE program offers young people the opportunity to learn by interacting with others.

Scenic Woods Branch Library, dedicated on October 19, 1986, serves a residential area in northeast Houston and is one of Houston Public Library's four regional libraries. The architectural firm, James Marshall Associates, created a custom-designed information center as the interior's focal point and a built-in puppet theater as the centerpiece for children's programming. Besides puppet shows, the branch offers a broad range of activities for children, including arts and crafts, story time, and movies. In response to an increase in the Hispanic population in the traditionally African-American community, the branch has added a large Spanish language collection. Super Neighborhood Council #47 provides strong support to Scenic Woods. When Scenic Woods closed for remodeling in late 2002, a temporary location opened in Tidwell Park Community Center.

After two decades of operating from the former W. L. Clayton home, called Clayton House, Houston Public Library built a larger library for genealogical research. Dedicated on October 29, 1988, the Clayton Library Center for Genealogical Research covers a two-block area in the heart of Houston's Museum District. As the second-largest public genealogical library in the United States, Clayton welcomes researchers from around the world. The library recognizes that there is a growing interest among the public in knowing about people—who they were, what they did, how they thought, and how they lived from day to day. Researchers access information through Clayton's non-circulating collection, which includes federal, state, county, and local records representing all fifty states and many foreign countries. Tours, lectures, workshops, and seminars are available to genealogical societies, civic groups, school classes, clubs, scout troops, as well as to individual genealogists. In 1987 Clayton Library Friends organized to support the library through contributions, special projects, and volunteer assistance.

Volunteers have always been one of the library's most valuable assets. In the early years, clubwomen gave many hours to the library by hosting events, preparing refreshments, serving on committees, and raising money. In the 1950s volunteers from the Ladies' Reading Club began compiling scrapbooks from the library's clippings on subjects related to Houston and Texas. It took the workers two years to complete these scrapbooks, which remain valuable tools for researchers. In more recent years, volunteers have assumed direct responsibility for assisting with library programming. Volunteer tutors work with students to improve their reading and math skills. In the branches, volunteers work at the information desk, shelve books, and assist with clerical work. Others find their niche teaching classes in computer training or in English-as-a-Second-Language. Some volunteers receive special training in processing library materials, and one spends hours each week rebinding books. A large corps of volunteers works all year on the Friends of the Public Library's annual book sale.

Long-term plans to build a Montrose branch at Richmond Avenue and Mandell Street changed when developer John Hansen donated the sanctuary of the former Central Church of Christ to the City of Houston in the spring of 1986. Ray Bailey, the architect responsible for the design of Hansen's adjacent Campanile project, converted architect William Ward Watkin's 1941 ecclesiastical design into a functional library. Bailey retained three key architectural elements–the bell tower, the tall windows, and the stained glass window–and added a second floor to provide more space. The library opened on March 5, 1988. Eleanor Freed, a longtime art critic of the *Houston Post* and a member of the Library Board, gave artwork to the library and established the Freed Endowment to be used to buy fine arts materials for the library. In 1995 Eleanor Freed's name was added to the name of the branch. Freed-Montrose Branch is an important resource for patrons using its rich art, theater, and literary collections, and it offers a diversity of programs, including book presentations, lectures, and story times. (Photo of Eleanor Freed courtesy Museum of Fine Arts, Houston Archives)

The Judson Robinson Jr.- Westchase Branch Library was dedicated on November 2, 1991, and opened to the public two days later. Its location in rapidly growing southwest Houston predicted that it would be one of the system's busiest branches. That prediction has materialized. For every full year that it has been open, Robinson-Westchase has been among the top three branches both in total circulation and in number of reference transactions. The branch was named for Judson Robinson Jr., the first African-American elected to Houston's City Council, a position to which he was re-elected nine times. The White Budd Van Ness Partnership designed the building. Robinson-Westchase Branch's patron base is a diverse mix, including businesspersons, retirees, students of all ages, and families with young children. To meet the needs and interests of these groups, the library offers the Summer Reading Program, Books for Babies Program, Parent Reading Program, and monthly computer classes. There are celebrations each year for African-American Heritage Month and Asian-American Heritage Month. It also maintains a strong working relationship with the Westchase Business District. (Photo of Judson Robinson Jr. courtesy of Margarette Robinson; photography by Kaye Marvins Photography, Inc.)

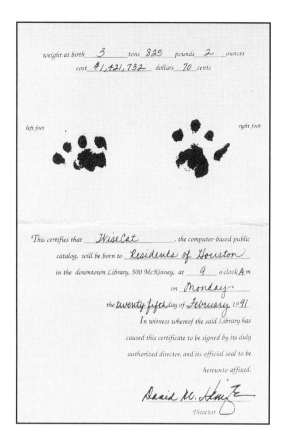

weight at birth _3_ tons _825_ pounds _2_ ounces
cost _$1,421,732_ dollars _70_ cents

left foot   right foot

This certifies that _WiseCat_ , the computer-based public
catalog, will be born to _Residents of Houston_
in the downtown Library, 500 McKinney, at _9_ o'clock _A_ m
on _Monday_
the _twenty-fifth_ day of _February_ 19 _91_
In witness whereof the said Library has
caused this certificate to be signed by its duly
authorized director, and its official seal to be
hereunto affixed.

David M. Henington
Director

Certificate of Birth

———— HOUSTON PUBLIC LIBRARY ————

On February 25, 1991, the Houston Public Library announced the birth of "Wise Cat," its first computer-based catalog system. A public awareness campaign urged patrons to dial up the library to meet "WiseCat," which weighed in at three tons and cost $1.5 million. "WiseCat" replaced the library's thirteen-year-old microfilm readers. It provided better and faster access to approximately 2.8 million listings and received monthly updates to incorporate new acquisitions. "WiseCat" also provided maps of library locations, floor plans, and a calendar of library events. In 1995 the library upgraded "WiseCat" from a CD-based system to an interactive online public access catalog, called OPAC. The OPAC system linked to the Internet, providing access not only to Houston Public Library's catalog, but also to other libraries and databases throughout the world. All the library branches also installed "Kid's Catalog," a children's version of OPAC. Walk-up online terminals significantly opened up the library's world of information to library users.

In 1995 Barbara A. B. Gubbin became the fifth person to direct the Houston Public Library. Gubbin received her Master of Arts in Library and Information Studies from the University of London and began her career in London, where she was the Director of the Fawcett Library. Upon moving to the United States, she joined the staff of the San Antonio Public Library. In 1989 Gubbin was named Assistant Director of the Houston system and became Director when David Henington retired in 1995. She took on the challenge of leading the library into the 21st century. Under her leadership, four new libraries have been constructed, including the first jointly-operated city-county facility. Twelve other libraries have undergone renovation, others are planned, and the Jesse Jones Building is currently initiating a $12 million renovation. Gubbin oversaw the design of "Standards for Excellence: A Master Plan for the Houston Public Library," approved by City Council in October 2003. This plan provides the basis for a study of the library services, facilities, technology, and organizational structure to guide the library system for the next decade. Like two of her predecessors—Julia Ideson and David Henington—Gubbin has served as president of the Texas Library Association. (Photograph by Barfield Photography Inc.)

In 1998 Mayor Lee P. Brown issued a challenge to the Houston Public Library and to the community when he decreed that every school-age child in Houston should have a library card. The library accepted the challenge and tackled the job of seeing that each of these children received the brightly colored library card. Schools, community organizations, corporations, local media, and city officials cooperated with library staff in reaching children all over the city. When the campaign ended, 303,000 Power cards had been issued to Houston's children. The Texas Library Association recognized the hard work, dedication, and enthusiasm of everyone involved when it chose the Power Card Challenge as the 1999 Project of the Year. A further honor came to the library when the American Library Association awarded it the John Cotton Dana Library Public Relations Award for the Power Card Challenge. The Power Card represents the potential to learn and to achieve offered to everyone through the resources provided by the Houston Public Library.

The Houston Public Library celebrated the opening of its thirty-fifth branch library on October 23, 1999, with a ribbon cutting by Mayor Lee P. Brown and presentations by celebrity story readers. The building, designed by Stoa International, sports a blue roof. It was named for prominent local attorney Sherman E. Stimley. The Stimley-Blue Ridge branch was the first Houston Public Library facility in Fort Bend County and fulfilled a longstanding commitment by the library system to provide service to the Blue Ridge community of southwest Houston. Since Stimley-Blue Ridge is near Briargate Elementary School, McAuliffe Middle School and Willowridge High School and is surrounded by day care centers, the library sponsors a variety of activities for children and teenagers. A community-wide Jamboree celebrates the conclusion of the Summer Reading Program. African-American Heritage Month has included programs on "History of Slave Quilts" and "Finding Your African-American Roots." In October 2002 the branch celebrated its 3rd anniversary with a Pajama Party.

Today computers are the backbone of the library system. Patrons use them for tasks as varied as searching the local library's catalog, writing school papers, and conducting research over the Internet. The computer interface with the World Wide Web enhances features in the catalog and provides access to information from all over the globe. To the library itself, the computer functions almost literally as a backbone. Through one integrated computer system, it maintains the library catalog, and manages circulation, selection, acquisition, and cataloguing of materials. In addition to functions that make the library services work, computers and data communications link users and staff to numerous licensed informational databases, the Internet, and office software. Even the library telephone system uses the Internet Protocol and shares the network communications line with the computers.

Parents now have a comfortable place to take all their parenting questions. In the spring of 1999, The Children's Museum of Houston, in partnership with the Houston Public Library, opened the Parent Resource Library in the museum. This unique facility is the first of its kind in the country. Nearly 1,000 visitors use the library each week, checking out books, thumbing through resources, and printing information off the Internet, while their children read books or play with educational toys alongside them. Materials in the library cover a broad range of parental concerns, including potty training, cultural issues, discipline, and a variety of special needs. The library maintains a referral list of local organizations and resources. Materials concerning discipline, ADHA, learning disabilities, and asthma are among the most popular items checked out. Resources are available in Spanish as well as English. By working together, the Houston Public Library and The Children's Museum of Houston are maintaining a cutting-edge resource center and establishing a model for other cities.

In 2002 the library initiated a partnership with the *Houston Chronicle* to develop a unique program, Books on the Bayou: Houston Reads Together. This collaboration sought to inspire reading and thoughtful discussion among Houstonians in libraries, classrooms, bookstores, coffee shops, or anywhere they happen to come together. The program centers on a single book, selected by a committee drawn from both the library and the community. The book selected the first year was *Lesson Before Dying* by Ernest Gaines, who made an appearance in Houston during the event. In 2003 the committee chose Ray Bradbury's *Farenheit 451*. Various groups hold events all over the city during the month-long program. Discussion groups, large and small, provide opportunity for an in-depth study of the reading. The Alley Theater has presented dramatic readings of the selected books, and the Museum of Fine Arts, Houston has participated by showing films based on them. Houstonians have responded enthusiastically to Books on the Bayou, and the Library and the *Houston Chronicle* continue to work to grow this annual event

When the Houston Lyceum and Carnegie Association received its charter in 1900, a Board of Trustees took on the responsibility of overseeing the Association's activities. That first board, comprised of nine citizens, guided the Association as it raised money for a site, hired a librarian, supervised the construction of a building, and implemented library policy. Since that time a board has continued to advise the Houston Public Library on the library's financial affairs, its physical properties, and other matters pertinent to the library's operation. Over time the board changed in composition, with the number of mayoral appointees ranging from seven to the present-day thirteen. The membership through the years is a distinguished list. Some individuals had long tenures on the board. Mrs. H. F. Ring served forty-one years; William A. Vinson served thirty-eight. Dr. Henry Barnston, Mrs. A. T. Carleton, and J. S. Bracewell were each members for more than twenty-five years. Members of the 2004 Library Board are seen here. They are: (front, left to right) Harriet Latimer, Lillie Robertson, Barbara A. B. Gubbin (Director), Zarine M. Boyce, Dr. J. S. Stone II; (back, left to right) Barry Hunsaker Jr., Dr. E. Fred Aguilar III, Saundria Chase Gray, Patricia J. Lasher, Miguel Espinosa, Franklin D. R. Jones Jr.; not pictured are James E. Bashaw, Jack S. Blanton Jr, and Ruth Ann Stimley.

A groundbreaking ceremony for the construction of the new Clear Lake City-County Freeman Branch Library was held on November 22, 2002. This branch represents the first joint library venture for the City of Houston and Harris County. Replacing the County Freeman Library, the new joint city-county structure maintains the name that commemorates Captain Theodore C. Freeman, the first astronaut to lose his life in the United States space program. The library, due to open in 2004, will have 160,000 items in its collection. It will be the largest branch in either library system. The children's area will be named "Betty's Place" in honor of Elizabeth "Betty" Ulrich, the founder and initial librarian of Clear Lake's first public library, who was also a volunteer at the Houston Public Library. Both the city and the county view this project as an opportunity to deliver to citizens a regional library housed in a state-of-the-art facility that will provide superior resource materials.

The most advanced technological facility within the Houston Public Library system will open in 2004. The John P. McGovern-Stella Link Branch Library is named to honor Dr. John P. McGovern, internationally renowned physician and generous philanthropist in support of many causes in Houston. The branch will become part of the McGovern-Stella Link Campus Park in southwest Houston. The once crime-infested area became a project of the Stella Link Redevelopment Association, whose goal was to provide a variety of services to the community. The 20,000-square-foot library building will house a Distance Learning Center that will include instructional television and interactive videoconferencing. Besides the traditional collections for adults, teens, and children, the library will include another first for the Houston Public Library system—an Internet Café with tables and ports for computer laptops. McGovern-Stella Link Branch Library will truly be a library for the 21st century. (Photo of Dr. John McGovern, courtesy Dr. McGovern)

In the first few months of 2004, Houston dedicated a sleek Metro light rail, turned on a spectacular fountain sculpture on Main Street, inaugurated its fifty-first mayor, spruced up to entertain the world at SuperBowl XXXVIII, and celebrated the 100th anniversary of the founding of the Houston Public Library. The juxtaposition of Houston's new look with the anniversary of its library underscores the close connections between the success of the city and its library system. Begun from the ambitions of early leaders to turn Houston into a world-class city, the Houston Public Library has continually matched the city's commitment to economic growth and support for a diverse population. One hundred years ago Houston leaders knew that a great city needed a great library. Together, Houston and its public library face the next century. (Photo courtesy Greater Houston Partnership)

SELECTED BIBLIOGRAPHY

Baron, Steven M. *Houston Electric: The Street Railways of Houston, Texas.* Lexington, Kentucky: Self published, 1995.

Cherry, Emma Richardson. Papers. Houston Metropolitan Research Center, Houston Public Library.

City Federation of Women's Clubs. Papers. Houston Metropolitan Research Center, Houston Public Library.

City Planning Commission. Report of the City Planning Commission, 1929.

Colored Carnegie Library Association. *Constitution and By-Laws Colored Carnegie Library.* Houston: Letheridge Printing, 1913.

Endelman, Sharon Bice. "Julia Bedford Ideson," *New Handbook of Texas, Vol. 3.* Austin: Texas State Historical Association, 1996.

Fall, Mrs. Henry, ed. *Key to the City of Houston.* Houston: State Publishing Co., 1908.

Finnigan. Collection. Houston Metropolitan Research Center, Houston Public Library.

Fox, Stephen and Drexel Turner, ed. *Lyceum to Landmark: The Julia Ideson Building of the Houston Public Library.* Houston: School of Architecture at Rice University and Friends of the Houston Public Library, 1979.

Gunter, Jewel Boone Hamilton. *Committed: The 100-Year History of the Woman's Club of Houston, 1893-1993.* Houston: D. Armstrong, Inc, 1995.

Hatch, Orin Walker. *Lyceum to Library: A Chapter in the Cultural History of Houston.* Texas Gulf Coast Historical Association, 1965.

Houston Lyceum and Carnegie Association. Annual Reports, 1904-1920.

Houston Public Library. Annual Reports, 1921-1995.

Houston Public Library. *The Handbook, Section 1.* Houston: Houston Public Library, 1962.

Houston Public Library. *Your Library: A Story of 25 Eventful Years.* Houston: Houston Public Library, 1951.

Houston Daily Post, March 13, 1899; January 9, 1900.

Houston Post, September 23, 1943; December 19, 1946; January 26, 1958; December 3, 1967.

Houston Republic, August 8, 1857.

Hudson, Estelle. "Houston Citizens Own Thousands of Books," *The Houstonian,* March 31, 1917.

Hurley, Marvin. *Decisive Years for Houston.* Houston: Houston Magazine, 1966.

Ideson, Julia. Papers. Houston Metropolitan Research Center, Houston Public Library.

Ladies' Reading Club. Collection. Houston Metropolitan Research Center, Houston Public Library.

Looscan, Adele Briscoe. Papers. Houston Metropolitan Research Center, Houston Public Library.

McComb, David. *Houston: A History.* Austin: University of Texas Press, 1981.

McDonald, Tom. *History of the Houston Fire Department.* Houston: Taylor Publishing Company, 1988.

McSwain, Mary Brown. "Julia Ideson, Houston Librarian 1880-1945." Master's thesis, University of Texas, 1966.

Ring, Elizabeth. Scrapbook. Houston Metropolitan Research Center, Houston Public Library.

Ring, Mrs. Roland. *Highlights of the History of the Ladies' Reading Club, 1885-1960.* Houston: Ladies' Reading Club, 1960.

Robinson, Lana. "Carnegie's Texas Legacy," *Texas Highways,* July 2003.

Tennessean. "Houston Library Gets Spacious New Home," March 4, 1976.

Texas Library Journal, March 1957.

Tsanoff, Corinne. *Neighborhood Doorways.* Houston: Neighborhood Centers Association, 1953.

Van Slyck, Abigail A. *Free to All: Carnegie Libraries and American Culture 1890-1920.* Chicago: University of Chicago Press, 1995.

Woman's Viewpoint, July 1, 1924.

Works Project Administration, Writers Program, compilers. *Houston: A History and Guide.* Houston: Anson Jones Press, 1942.